PERSEVERANCE.
REINVENTION.

ANN SCHREIBER

PERSEVERANCE.
REINVENTION.

Losing it All to Gain
What Really Matters

FOX
POINTE
PUBLISHING

This book is a memoir. It contains the author's present memories of experiences
over time. Some names have been changed, some events have been condensed, and
some dialogue has been recreated.

www.foxpointepublishing.com/author-ann-schreiber

Library of Congress Cataloging-in-Publication Data
Schreiber, Ann, author.
Town, Scotty, designer.
Perseverance. Reinvention. / Ann Schreiber. – First edition.
Summary: This book equips the reader with the understanding and tools to embrace change and
craft a fulfilling new life.
ISBN (softcover) 978-1-955743-09-9
[1. Memoirs – Biography & Autobiography. 2. Divorce & Separation – Family & Relationships.
3. Personal Growth – Self-Help.]
Library of Congress Control Number: 2 0 2 4 9 5 1 4 0 2

Printed and bound in the United States of America
First printing December 2024

PREFACE

To My Readers,

First, if you are reading this book and have no idea who I am—thank you. You are who I am hoping to reach. I am so grateful that you're taking a chance on me, reading my story, and hopefully learning just a tidbit or two that can help you with your own perseverance and reinvention.

And I want to offer a few words here before we get into things. Many people have been attributed to the famous saying that there are three sides to every story. Regardless of who said it the first time, there is serious weight to the meaning behind those words—three sides to every story.

It's human nature to want to be right. But our memories are only so strong and so accurate. And we're human. So, often, we interpret things in our own ways, usually to protect us from the reality of what has actually happened.

This book is intended to be my story. I may mention others, but they have their own stories to tell. This one is mine—it's my version of various events that have transpired in my life. And if I can help one ordinary woman going through an ordinary challenge, my book will be a success. While this book is a reflection of my perseverance and my reinvention, I hope it can guide you on your own path to the same.

Thank you.

INTRODUCTION

IF I TOLD YOU THAT I HAD BEEN SITTING on this topic for years and years, I'd be lying to you. In fact, the idea just popped into my head recently, like when you find that missing sock hiding behind the dryer. The light bulb moment, you know? I started sharing my story with more and more people, and they'd say things like, "A lesser person wouldn't survive what you went through," or "You're the epitome of perseverance," and even, "You've totally reinvented yourself."

But I did sit on this topic for a while because I wondered, who would care about an ordinary woman like me? I'm not a celebrity; I'm not rolling in dough. I'm just a regular person with regular problems. Plus, I hesitated because I know people who've been through way worse. I've met folks who've lost their children, battled unemployment for months, or faced challenges that would make my worst days look like a picnic.

But you know what? I've endured some things that have given me the courage to tell this story. I hope my experiences can show you that, no matter how tough things get, you can persevere, become a better version of yourself, learn from the darkest times, and emerge stronger.

Now, I won't sugarcoat it. Life hasn't always been a walk in the park for me. There were days when I wondered why I'd even get out of bed. Why did I deserve the pain I went through? Why did I lose a baby during the second trimester of pregnancy? And why did my husband, who I'd been with for 23 years, deceive me and start a new life with someone he'd pushed me to befriend? Remember how Princess Diana said there were three people in her marriage? Yeah, I get it. That happened to me, too.

And why did my husband look at me one day as I sobbed in the bathroom, wondering what went wrong, only to tell me he felt disdain toward me? What type of husband does that? Especially after I'd stood by him through thick and thin. I won't spill all the beans here to protect the guilty, but believe me, he put me through the wringer. I stuck by him when he made terrible decisions, yelled at our kids, and forgot to pick them up from school, leaving them feeling like their dad didn't care. Let me tell you, marriage to him was no cakewalk. But I loved him. Anyway, we'll get into that more in another chapter.

Now, let's talk about what this book is about and why it matters to you and anyone else who needs a little inspiration while trying to piece their life back together.

In the immortal words of Aibileen to Mae Mobley in the fantastic film "The Help":

"You is kind. You is smart. You is important."

I am kind. I am intelligent. And I am important.

Say those words with me, will you? "I am kind, I am intelligent, and I am important." No matter what you've been through, you can take it and turn it into something incredible. You can go from losing everything to having it all. And the second time around, it can be even better than the first.

But let's back up a bit and let me introduce myself properly. I'm Ann Schreiber, and I have two amazing adult children, Cate and Zach. As of the rerelease of this book, my daughter is persevering as a psychotherapist-counselor for a local faith-based counseling organization. Her goal is to help others believe in themselves and persevere through life's obstacles.

Her husband is studying to be a pharmacist. Nathan has been such an amazing light in our lives, and I am so happy he is part of our family. After all, he chose my daughter because she's pretty amazing, and I couldn't agree more.

My son Zach graduated from college, obtained his teaching license, and started his first full-time teaching job as a special education teacher at a nearby middle school. His passion is helping kids persevere despite learning disabilities.

My kids are doing great things in the world. And as you can imagine, I'm one proud momma. But the truth is that I've learned a ton from my kids, especially in the last five years. But enough about them; I'll talk about them plenty in the chapters to come.

In January 2023, I experienced a layoff, and surprisingly, it turned out to be one of the best things that ever happened to me. The company I worked for had a toxic culture, especially among the leadership team. Have you ever been on a Zoom call and wondered what those chuckles on the other side of the camera were about? Yeah, the leadership team would exchange messages, poking fun at some of the attendees, including me. I mean, seriously, I thought adults would be above that kind of behavior, but let me tell you, it exists. So, leaving that place was a blessing in disguise.

Of course, when I got the news, I had a few moments of panic. I cried, I freaked out. But it didn't take long, and I mean hours, not days before I realized I was better than what that company could offer to me. I had more to offer the world. I could do better and achieve more. Sure, I went through the rounds of interviews with different companies. Thankfully, my resumé was up-to-date, and I had a pretty robust LinkedIn profile, so networking wasn't a problem.

However, over the next week or so, during countless interviews (probably around a dozen), I started hearing the same things repeatedly: "Your income expectations are too high... Your previous titles are too senior (vice president, director, etc.), and we need someone more junior... Your skills are out of date." And the one that finally opened my eyes: "Your specialty is in content, but we need someone who can do more than just content."

And then it hit me: content. In this case, content meant writing—business blogs, articles, landing pages, email campaigns, you name it. That was my specialty, my passion. I could get lost in words on a page, writing for hours. In fact, my ability to communicate through writing was way better than my verbal skills.

Now, it's important to know that I'd been freelancing on the side since 2017, really ramping it up in 2019. I had a handful of clients. So, when the layoff came (my fourth in my 30-year career), I had a eureka moment. Could I turn that side hustle into something more significant? Could it become a full-time gig?

But I won't spill all the beans just yet.

I hope this gives you a taste of what's to come. I've been through four layoffs, divorce, and infidelity, the loss of a baby during the second trimester of pregnancy, the near-loss of my son (I'll save that story for later), and losing pretty much everything I had. In the end, I rediscovered myself. I'll never be the same as I once was, and parts of me are still healing, still learning to persevere and get through the day. Yet I feel it is time to tell my story because I want others to come along on the road with me. To find strength, healing, and a future of happiness and comfort.

So, what exactly does persevering mean? If you asked Dictionary.com, it would tell you that perseverance means continuing a course of action, even when things are tougher than a two-dollar steak, with little or no chance of success. Okay, that's not exactly what it says. But you get my point. And the thing is that you can persevere, overcome even the darkest moments, and emerge stronger on the other side.

And what's this reinvention thing all about? Reinventing yourself is like giving yourself a fabulous makeover. It's taking the fantastic parts of who you are and making them even better. It's about discovering facets of yourself that you never knew existed. It's about learning from your mistakes and rising above them. It's about becoming a better version of yourself—one that can pick up the pieces, move forward, and create a downright fantastic life.

One thing's for sure: I've chosen perseverance. I've chosen reinvention. And let me tell you, the light at the end of the tunnel is blindingly bright. It can be for you, too.

The
Life
I Thought
I Knew

THE EARLY YEARS

LET'S START AT THE VERY BEGINNING—childhood. My early years were about as ordinary as they come. I wasn't raised in a house of horrors. I grew up in the Twin Cities suburbs in a regular, upper-middle-class family. I had everything I needed and a fair share of what I wanted. My mom wore many hats, including being my Girl Scout leader, soccer coach and more. She was the super woman who juggled being a stay-at-home mom and later returned to college in her 40s to become a nurse. Dad, on the other hand, was a driven entrepreneur who imparted valuable life skills, like tech know-how, professional etiquette, and the art of customer care.

From these two, I learned some lifelong skills that I still use today. Sure, my family wasn't the overly affectionate type, showering us with hugs, kisses, and "I love yous." But I always knew I was loved. I was fortunate.

My dad, always tech-savvy, brought home an Apple computer when it became affordable, and that moment changed the trajectory of my life. Up until then, I'd been into writing fictional short stories. I was that kid who despised the playground during recess. Not into tag or sports, I preferred indoor days playing board games or scribbling away in my notebook.

You'd find me, most likely, with my back to the school building, writing away with one of those stackable lead pencils (remember those?).

When the computer arrived, my dad introduced me to word processing. He showed me the keyboard, and that was it. I was hooked. The catch? I didn't know how to type—not yet–and I had no clue how to translate my thoughts from my head onto the computer screen. But I was a pro at putting words on paper.

Time and practice, however, worked their magic, and I figured it out. A new hobby was born. When I wasn't scribbling in my diary or jotting down short stories in my notebooks, I was glued to that computer. It was my solace, my happy place. Writing made me feel at peace.

This passion stayed with me. In middle school, I joined the school yearbook and newspaper teams. Recess meant interviewing anyone, even the intimidating school principal. While I can't recall what those middle school articles were about now, I remember the empowerment I felt while conducting interviews. Telling a good story was my jam.

High school brought a similar trajectory. I eagerly joined the high school paper, known as "Irish Impressions." I started as a regular reporter, writing whatever the situation called for. My sophomore year, I continued as a reporter, and by junior year, I was the news editor.

As I approached college, I began thinking about my future and beefing up my GPA and course list. Let me tell you, I despised math, science, physical education, history, and anything that didn't involve books or writing. So, when it came to choosing electives, I loaded up on those that allowed me to do what I loved. By the time I graduated high school, I had probably taken every English course offered. I just couldn't get enough.

Speaking of typing, remember how Dad introduced me to computers? Well, as a young teen, I taught myself to type and was blazing through more than one hundred words per minute. When high school required a typing class, I protested. Why sit in a class relearning what I already knew?

Dad took up my cause and contacted the school. They agreed that I could skip the class if I passed a typing test. Not only did I pass, but I typed faster and more accurately than the instructor. This little anecdote helps explain why I'm so comfortable hiding behind a computer screen, typing away at all hours. The words simply flowed.

In my senior year, I became the editor-in-chief. Simultaneously, I entered a post-secondary education program. I spent the first trimester at the high school, and for the next two, I attended a local junior college. This program allowed me to explore journalism and take more writing courses than my high school offered. It was also financially practical, since no college fund was waiting for me. I was already a college sophomore by the time I graduated high school.

It was an incredible experience. I juggled college coursework with high school newspaper responsibilities, and my high school experience prepared me to become the co-editor-in-chief of the junior college paper during my sophomore year. I soaked up valuable lessons, mastering the skills I'd learned in high school. I learned about "above the fold" and "below the fold," what a "lede" was, and how to frame up an article. Conducting interviews and capturing the essence of a story became second nature.

I fast-tracked through junior college, earning my Associate of Arts in General Studies. I transferred to the University of Minnesota for my junior year, gearing up to enter journalism school. I dedicated countless hours to preparing my entrance essay and taking the G-MAT exam, one of the prerequisites for the University of Minnesota's journalism program. I secured glowing letters of recommendation from my high school and junior college newspaper advisors. I checked all the boxes.

Hard work paid off; I got in. I started taking journalism courses, and it was challenging. I thought I knew everything but quickly realized there was still much to learn. Luckily, I paid attention and persevered, even while working full time as a manager for a major electronics retailer.

Then, during my second trimester at journalism school, disturbing rumors spread like wildfire. They said our journalism school would lose its accreditation. I didn't fully understand the implications, but it didn't sound good. So I changed my major. After all the effort to get into journalism school, I switched to an English major. Writing remained my passion, but English and communication studies had different requirements.

I was thrilled that I could still write, but a void had opened up within me. I was no longer on the path I'd envisioned—becoming an investigative reporter and journalist. And around the end of my junior year, in July 1995, I met the man who would become my first husband. I hadn't expected that or what would come of the relationship.

LIFE BEFORE THE DIVORCE

MY FIRST HUSBAND, who I'll refer to as Ryan, and I met in July of 1995. We were both working for an electronics retailer in the Twin Cities. He had relocated to the Twin Cities from a Chicago suburb about a year before we met and was a sales manager. I was an operations supervisor, soon to be promoted to manager.

Our initial connection was strong. He asked me out within a day or two of meeting, and we hit it off. Before long, he mentioned the idea of buying a townhouse in the area and asked if I was interested in moving in with him. This posed a tough decision for me as I was unsure how my parents would feel about me cohabiting with a partner. However, I was fiercely independent and eager to live on my own. Despite my parents having built an additional sub-level to their home for me to reside in during my college years and beyond, I felt constrained. While they didn't impose many rules at that point, I yearned for autonomy.

Within a few weeks we were in the process of building a townhouse in a St. Paul suburb. By Christmas of 1995, we were living together. And by February 1996, we were engaged. It was a whirlwind romance. Though we enjoyed each other's company and had fun together, looking back now, things weren't always as rosy as they seemed.

I want to acknowledge here that I understand I probably should have left the relationship. There were countless instances of tears and discontent, yet I remained. However, it wasn't all bleak. He was ambitious, and I admired that about him. He was always striving for success in his career, and I, too, was ambitious and wanted to achieve the best I could. Together, we were a dynamic duo on the rise. Why would I walk away from that?

So I persevered. We exchanged vows on September 6, 1997, in the presence of our loved ones. I took my vows seriously, grounded in my faith in God, although I didn't—and still don't—openly discuss my religious beliefs or my personal relationship with God. That said, standing in that church, surrounded by dear ones, I was committed to making the marriage work, no matter what challenges arose.

Unfortunately, the honeymoon phase faded quickly. As the days went on, I started learning more about Ryan's quirks, and even more so, his vices. Many of them seemed to come out of nowhere. But I had made a commitment to our marriage, and I made the commitment to stand by him.

And this was just the beginning. We suffered a devastating miscarriage in early 1999, and quite honestly, I am not sure our marriage was ever the same after that. We were so young to go through what we did. The pain, both physical for me and emotional for both of us, was nearly overpowering. We didn't know how to support one another through it. I felt abandoned by him, and I am sure he felt abandoned by me. Our forms of grieving were different, and we never did figure out how to get in sync to help each other through.

Just a few short months after the miscarriage, we embarked on trying to conceive again. In early June 1999, we received the news: we were expecting once more. Still, my joy was tinged with apprehension this time. I found it difficult to fully embrace the pregnancy, haunted by memories of our previous loss. How could I bond with this new baby when my heart still ached for the one we had lost? It was a tangled web of emotions to navigate.

At my ten-week appointment, when the doctor once again struggled to detect a heartbeat, my world teetered on the brink of collapse. This time, however, the doctor's determination matched my own desperation. She called in a more experienced physician, who eventually unearthed the rhythmic thump of our baby's heart. It was a moment of pure relief and elation.

As it turned out, I had a condition known as anterior placenta, where the placenta attaches to the front of the uterus. Though not cause for concern, it explained the difficulty in detecting the heartbeat during those early weeks.

At our mid-term ultrasound, we discovered we were having a girl. While I would have been thrilled either way, the prospect of a daughter filled me with excitement. Despite not being particularly girly myself growing up, I envisioned all the glittering dresses, flowing hair, and more that awaited us. (Thankfully, my daughter would fulfill those dreams in the years to come).

With each passing day of my pregnancy, I couldn't shake the fear of another loss. Despite being labeled "high risk" due to the previous miscarriage, the pregnancy progressed smoothly, albeit with some additional appointments and monitoring.

On March 15, 2000, my blood pressure soared due to undiagnosed pre-eclampsia. Yet, the very next day, my daughter entered the world, her arrival marked by a mix of relief and trepidation. Though her birth was marred by the urgency of my high blood pressure and her subsequent brief stay in the NICU, she was perfect in every way. Both Ryan and I fell deeply in love with her from the moment we laid eyes on her—a love that would only grow with time.

Fast forward to May 23, 2002, and we welcomed our son into the world. However, this pregnancy was fraught with challenges. At just thirty weeks, I went into preterm labor, requiring weeks of bed rest to delay his arrival. When my blood pressure spiked again, this time dangerously, our son was delivered prematurely. Despite the rocky start, he, too, was flawless as far as I was concerned—a beautiful addition to our family.

With the arrival of our son, our family felt complete. This sentiment was reinforced by a sobering conversation with my doctor, who expressed concerns about my health following multiple pregnancy complications. Ryan and I agreed that two children were enough. Our family was indeed complete.

And while these occasions were joyous, there will always be a feeling of bitterness mixed in. The details really don't matter, but Ryan made some poor decisions in our marriage—and he made them multiple times.

The truth is, I could go on for pages recounting all that I endured during those years. But it would be an entire book in itself. And this is not a book meant to berate him or paint him as a bad person. The fact is he had demons and, as far as our marriage was concerned, those demons were discovered a little too late. And what I truly want this book to be about is perseverance and reinvention, about picking yourself up each time life knocks you down, praying that it won't get worse.

But let me be clear: while this chapter may have originally been written as an exposé on my ex-husband, I was not entirely blameless in the demise of our marriage. I had grown distant, as he often pointed out. And he was right—I had lost my attraction to him. How could I be attracted to someone who had done the things he had done?

He became unappealing to me, and I'm sure he felt emasculated, stripped of his role and identity as a man. His irresponsible behavior and actions made him no longer resemble a husband but rather a man-child in my bed.

And that's just the way it was. Our marriage endured, though perhaps "survived" is a more fitting term. It felt like we were two separate entities, almost like business partners, with one carrying the weight (that would be me).

Has this ever happened to you? What actions do you see in the person you love that cause you to turn away? How do you communicate those feelings and work toward change? Write down your thoughts at the end of this chapter.

But in 2017, visible cracks began to appear. We started socializing with another couple, long-time friends of my ex. As our children grew old enough to stay home alone, we'd spend weekends with this couple at our cabin, as it was a good "half-way" point from where they lived to our home south of the river in the Twin Cities. While the men fished and tinkered with boats, the women played Scrabble, mixed cocktails, and swam. I didn't think much of it until we planned a joint vacation—a two-week cruise to South America. Ryan suggested inviting this couple along, and I agreed without hesitation.

As the cruise approached, I noticed Ryan frequently mentioning the other woman. Her name seemed to crop up in more and more conversations. Then, during the cruise, I observed that when Ryan wasn't around, neither was she. It seemed odd, but I brushed it off until my daughter remarked, "Why are we always playing board games with her husband? And why is she never here when Dad isn't?"

My daughter's observation alarmed me, but seemed to confirm my suspicions. When Norovirus struck the ship, leaving me bedridden, Ryan chose to spend his time dancing with this other couple rather than caring for me. And by the end of the cruise, they announced their divorce. They had come on the cruise, not wanting to lose their money. Yet, their marriage had been over before the cruise had begun.

After we returned home from the cruise, the dynamic shifted. Ryan encouraged a closer friendship between me and the other woman, but her behavior raised red flags. I won't list them here, but I'll tell you this—have you ever Googled signs that your partner might be cheating on you? Have you ever taken to your favorite search engine to understand the differences between emotional and physical infidelity? Try it sometime—it's fascinating, to say the least.

So let's fast forward to how in December 2018, I pulled up in my best friend's driveway one evening, having texted her before my arrival, telling her to meet me outside. I rolled down my window, looked at her, and demanded reassurance that my husband wasn't having an affair. Of course, her reaction was to deny my concerns. But I took her through the evidence—the pages and pages I had collected over the recent months. By the time I had reached the end of my list, she couldn't deny the possibility.

Though he never confessed, mounting evidence and my children's observations convinced me otherwise. I proposed marriage counseling, which we attended from February to July 2019. But in our final session, he declared he no longer wanted to be married. Fueled by anger and disbelief, I expelled him from my life—or at least as much as one can when you share two children together.

To summarize, I had remained committed to our vows and our marriage through it all—until he wasn't.

Have you ever felt stuck in something because you agreed to do it, then realized you made a mistake? What did you do? How did you get out of it? Are you stuck in a bad situation today? Take a moment to reflect on what you have learned from the situation and what you can do to move forward.

COPING WITH MISCARRIAGE

I WANT TO GO BACK TO SOMETHING I talked about in the last chapter. I want to take the opportunity to fully honor the loss I experienced as well as the similar losses others have experienced.

Navigating that early second-trimester miscarriage in 1999 was a tough journey. Deciding whether to talk about it was hard, too. Last year, my son lost a close friend in a bad car crash. I think about that boy often, devastated for his parents, devastated for my son and all those who were blessed to have him in their life.

The truth is that I've seen too many parents lose their kids over the years—to cancer, other sicknesses, accidents, and more. So, a part of me feels bad writing about my miscarriage.

According to the March of Dimes, about 10 to 20 pregnancies out of 100 end in miscarriage. Most miscarriages, about 8 out of 10, happen in the first trimester before the 12th week. Miscarriages in the second trimester, between 13 and 19 weeks, happen in 1 to 5 pregnancies out of 100. When it happens after 20 weeks, it's called a stillbirth.

That's a lot of babies who never got to take their first breath or be held in their parents' arms. It's sad thinking about all the things they never got to do.

There's a weird feeling about talking about miscarriages. Some people think it's not a big deal because the baby was never born. But it's a big deal for those who've been through it. When you find out you're pregnant, you start dreaming about the baby's future.

Perhaps this is why it hurts so much. So many people, especially those who have never experienced it, tend to think that we should "just get over it." After all, there are parents out there who have gone through so much worse.

The baby I lost in miscarriage was real for me, and I believe many others who have gone through a similar experience feel the same. The moment that pregnancy test showed a positive result, or the nurse delivered the news after a blood draw (in my case), hopes and dreams for that child began to form. Thoughts of bringing them home from the hospital, designing their nursery, envisioning their first day of school, high school graduation, college drop-off, buying their first car, and even imagining their wedding day flooded my mind.

I can vividly recall pondering all of these milestones. While I may not have felt entirely ready to embrace motherhood when my ex expressed his desire to start a family, I can assure you that the day I learned I was pregnant, I was more than 1000% ready.

Then came the cramps and the sight of blood on the toilet paper, shattering those dreams in an instant. Though I hadn't fully recognized that something was amiss before that moment in the bathroom, looking back, I began to piece together subtle signs from the weeks prior. My expanding belly no longer carried the same sensitivity to the smell of cooking meat. That nausea that had greeted me each morning faded away, and even the slight "morning sickness" I experienced in the evenings disappeared.

The confirmation from the radiologist marked the beginning of a profound emotional turmoil. To be honest, I'm not certain if the wounds from that day have ever fully healed. While the intensity of the pain has lessened over time, remnants of it still linger beneath the surface.

In retrospect, I believe the loss of this baby was the harbinger of the end of my marriage. The emotional anguish I endured left my ex unsure of how to provide support. While he, too, experienced devastation, he seemed to move on from his pain relatively quickly. For me, however, it persisted.

I sought solace in therapy and conversations with friends, yet only those who had walked a similar path could truly understand the depth of my grief. In sharing my experience, I hope to provide some measure of comfort to others, just as they have done for me.

So, what's the message here? While I pray that you never have to endure the heartache of a miscarriage or the loss of a child, if you do, know that you don't have to suffer in silence. There are people who will listen, including myself. I'll offer you that embrace, lend an ear, and stand by you as you revisit that fateful day year after year.

But I assure you that you will find the strength to persevere. You'll weather the storm, you'll emerge resilient. Yet, it's essential to acknowledge that you'll never forget. And that's perfectly okay. Your baby deserves a place in your memories, and your story deserves to be heard by anyone willing to listen.

Have you lost a child during miscarriage? Have you been trying to get pregnant with no luck? Take a moment to share your thoughts and honor your lost baby here.

Grief

.

THE PAINFUL DIVORCE

DIVORCE IS A PAIN UNLIKE ANY OTHER, one I wouldn't wish upon my worst enemy.

The emotions are overwhelming—sadness, anger, exhaustion, frustration, confusion—they consume you. And the anxiety about the uncertain future adds another layer of fear. Even if the relationship was toxic, stepping into the unknown is terrifying.

For me, devastation doesn't even begin to describe it. As the end neared, before that fateful day at the therapist's office, I found myself alone in the master bathroom at our cabin, tears streaming down my face in despair. It had been months since my ex had shown any affection, and it seemed like he was actively avoiding me. When he finally came in to check on me, his words cut like a knife. "I just look at you with disdain," he said.

His ignorance of the meaning of the word didn't lessen the blow. How could he, after everything, regard me with such contempt? It felt like my heart had been ripped out.

The following months passed in a blur. I had kept the number of a divorce attorney for years, teetering on the edge of calling him. But I remained dedicated to our marriage until I realized that commitment was one-sided.

Driving home from the therapy session where our marriage had effectively ended, I made the call I had been avoiding. By Monday morning, I had an appointment scheduled with the attorney. My priority was protecting myself and my children, especially my youngest, who was about to start his senior year of high school.

The divorce papers were served on July 15, 2019. In them, I insisted that my ex disable all tracking devices he had placed on my phone, my car, and the security cameras at the cabin—a violation of privacy that had plagued me throughout the marriage. Ladies (or gentlemen), if you find yourself being monitored by someone who claims to love you—this is not an act of love. It is an act of control. Don't let yourself be monitored (and subsequently, don't engage in activities where your partner would feel the need to do so). Anyway, I digress.

I went through the stages of divorce like a whirlwind:

- Denial faded quickly; the signs of his emotional infidelity were too glaring to ignore.
- Anger simmered just beneath the surface like a constant companion that I couldn't get to leave.
- Bargaining seemed pointless; there was nothing left to negotiate.
- Depression weighed heavily on my shoulders, threatening to drown me.
- Acceptance was a distant goal, one I struggled to grasp.

The anger remained—sharp and relentless. I lost everything in that divorce, save for my children. And within days of the separation, I knew I had to sell our home. The financial burden was too heavy to bear alone.

And the reminders of that woman who had spent time in our home—slept in our guest room—were memories that would haunt me.

The decision about our cabin in northern Minnesota weighed heavily on me. It held so many cherished memories, but the practicality of maintaining it as a single parent was overwhelming. Ultimately, I had to let it go, along with everything it represented. And so I would need to rebuild, from the very bottom, and work my way back to the proverbial top.

Despite my perception of strength, the word "disdain" echoed in my mind, a heavy burden on my already aching heart. How could someone I had invested so much love and trust in regard me with such contempt? How could someone feel that way about me after I had stood by his side, through all those infractions? The pain cut deep, leaving wounds that seemed impossible to heal.

I must confront a truth that is often shrouded in silence: there were moments when the pain became unbearable and when the darkness threatened to consume me. Suicidal ideations crept into my mind, whispering promises of escape from the relentless pain I felt every day. There were times that the weight of existence felt too heavy to bear.

I was nearly 45 years old, married since the age of 22, and with the same partner since I was just 20. That's a lifetime of dedication, of nurturing a relationship that now lay shattered at my feet. What purpose did I serve in a world where my worth was questioned and my existence felt meaningless? Doubts gnawed at my soul—was I truly capable of being the mother my children needed? Had I failed them too?

Each morning brought a new battle as I fought to rise from my bed, the weight of despair holding me down. Nights were plagued with nightmares and it was impossible to sleep. Nausea and this pressure in my chest became a constant companion, a relentless reminder of my shattered reality. I felt like I was lost at sea, just a shell of the person I once was.

Yet, even when I felt surrounded by darkness, I knew it wasn't worth it to let it consume me. Ryan wasn't worth it. I knew I was worth so much more. I'm smart. I'm driven and motivated. And I have a big heart filled with love for those who are part of my life.

It was like this soft whisper in my ear saying, "You can overcome this." There was a possibility for resilience, even redemption. So, in the depths of despair, I discovered a strength I never knew existed—a resilience coming to light through those ashes of despair.

Though each day became a battle, getting through was a daily testament to my will to survive. Through the tears and the pain, I found solace in the love of my children. They were my bright lights in all of that darkness. Their unwavering faith in me reignited a flicker of hope, a reminder that even in my darkest moments, I was not alone.

As I navigated through the grief and loss, I began to reclaim my sense of self. Piece by broken piece, I stitched together the fragments of my shattered heart, forging a new path. Yes, the journey was fraught with setbacks and obstacles including a doozy that I'll tell you about later. But, with each step forward, I grew stronger.

Though the scars of my past may never fully fade, they serve as a reminder of the battles I've fought and the strength I've gained. I have since emerged not unscathed, but resilient—a testament to the indomitable human spirit. I have and will continue to persevere.

NAVIGATING THE EMOTIONAL TOLL OF DIVORCE

GOING THROUGH A DIVORCE is a life-altering experience that often comes with a whirlwind of emotions. It's a journey I never anticipated taking, yet here I am. The shock and disbelief of it all still linger, even years after the final papers were signed. What stings the most is the realization that the person I stood by through thick and thin, the one I dedicated myself to, ultimately chose to walk away and pursue another relationship.

The toll of the divorce weighed heavily on me, leaving me feeling unworthy, undeserving, and downright ugly. The word "disdain" echoed in my mind, a constant reminder of how little regard my ex-husband seemed to have for me. How could someone I loved and supported for so long treat me with such contempt?

If you find yourself facing the prospect of divorce, know that you are not alone. While statistics may not offer much comfort, the truth is that countless others have navigated this path and emerged stronger on the other side. Perseverance is key, and, though the road may be rocky, there is light at the end of the tunnel.

Here are some insights I gained as I weathered the emotional storm of divorce:

- Recognize Your Feelings: It's okay to experience a range of emotions, from shock and denial to anger and depression. Allow yourself to feel without judgment.

- Give Yourself Grace: Be kind to yourself during this challenging time. You're doing the best you can, and that's enough.

- Seek Support: Don't go through this alone. Reach out to friends, family, or a therapist who can provide comfort and guidance.

- Honor Your Feelings: Suppressing your emotions will only prolong the healing process. Allow yourself to express how you're feeling, whether it's through journaling, talking, or creative outlets.

- Embrace Change: Moving on may seem intimidating and downright scary, but remember that it's the ultimate goal. Focus on building a fulfilling life for yourself, one step at a time.

- Acknowledge the Five Stages of Divorce: Shock and Denial, Anger, Bargaining, Depression, and Acceptance are not linear stages; they may occur in a different order and intensity for each individual. That's definitely been the case for me, and I am often surprised when, even today, they can rear their ugly heads.

Navigating the emotional toll of divorce is similar to mourning a loss. The intensity of this period often peaks within the first six months of separation but may persist for up to two years. In my case, it's been over four years since my divorce. While I've remarried and found love again, there are still days when the pain resurfaces, leaving me questioning what went wrong. And more so, leading me to a conversation with God, pleading that He not let this marriage fail, too.

Entering into a new relationship or marriage can be especially intimidating, as past wounds may linger, casting a shadow of doubt on the future. It's natural to wonder how someone new can love you differently from your previous spouse and whether history will repeat itself.

While statistics may paint a grim picture of second marriages, it's essential to acknowledge their unique challenges. Lingering resentments, shared financial obligations, and blended families can strain even the strongest relationships. In my case, blending our families presented its own set of challenges, as my husband and I had children from my previous marriage and his previous relationship, and those kids had different needs and priorities.

To prioritize the success of a remarriage, putting your new relationship first, addressing past issues, and creating open communication are non-negotiables. Additionally, building positive relationships with stepchildren and addressing conflicts early on can help prevent larger problems down the road.

Here are some things that I do to help keep my current marriage strong and to make it a priority.

EXPRESSING LOVE DAILY

I make it a priority to express my love to my husband daily, often multiple times. While he understands my feelings, verbalizing them strengthens our bond and builds closeness. Likewise, he reciprocates, understanding my need to hear those words.

Why is this daily affirmation so important to me? Reflecting on my upbringing, I realized that verbal expressions of love were rare in my family. Though I felt loved, hearing those words was equally important. When I became a parent, I made it a point to break this pattern, ensuring my children heard "I love you" daily, reinforcing our emotional connection.

In my previous marriage, verbal expressions of love were infrequent, a subtle warning sign in hindsight. However, my current marriage has taught me the true depth of love. My husband is my rock, my lifelong partner who I pray will be by my side until my end of days. I see my love reflected in his eyes, and hearing those words exchanged daily adds sweetness to our relationship, affirming our bond.

MORNING EMBRACE RITUAL

I prioritize sharing a morning hug with my husband. It's all about the significance of physical touch for me, especially at the start of the day. Given that physical affection was lacking in my previous relationship, I now value it immensely.

Why does this daily ritual matter? Among the hustle and bustle of daily life, it's easy to lose sight of what truly matters. These morning embraces are essential as someone whose love language includes physical touch. Despite our differing schedules, we make sure to take time before lunch to share this meaningful gesture, accompanied by a loving smile. Each hug revitalizes me, infusing my day with positivity and warmth.

ALLOCATING QUALITY TIME

Carving out quality time for each other alongside our busy schedules is indeed a challenge. Despite my passion for nighttime writing and his enjoyment of television and video games, we make it a priority to spend at least two evenings a week together. Moreover, we aim for a monthly date night to deepen our connection.

Quality time together doesn't always require a formal outing, however. It can be as simple as watching a TV show together, enjoying each other's company while pursuing our individual interests, or even going grocery shopping as a duo—though I truly despise grocery shopping, so when I opt to go along, it is truly a testament of my love for him.

The key is being present and engaged in dialogue, cherishing those moments of togetherness and fostering our bond. Whether it's a planned date night or an impromptu evening at home, these shared experiences strengthen our relationship and reinforce our commitment to each other.

NON-PHYSICAL INTIMACY

Intimacy extends beyond physical closeness. While cuddling plays a significant role in creating emotional connection, it's just one part of the equation.

I know I can go on and on about all this, but I want to keep this section brief because this book isn't primarily about intimacy or the intricacies of my personal relationship with my husband. However, it's essential to acknowledge the profound impact of non-physical intimacy in strengthening the emotional connection between partners. It's about that time you spend talking, running errands, or just being in the same room together. When you and your partner share a deep friendship and invest time in each other, the intimacy that blossoms can be truly remarkable.

RESPECTING FAMILY TIME

We both understand the significance of spending quality time with our respective children. To accommodate this, I arrange nights out with my friends on occasion when his daughter is home, allowing him to enjoy father-daughter time. Likewise, he supports my desire to have occasional outings with my kids alone. By respecting each other's parental roles and autonomy, we strengthen our bond as a couple and as parents.

The practices listed above contribute to the foundation of our marriage, encouraging love, understanding, and mutual respect. Through consistent effort and communication, we're learning to navigate the complexities of life together, ensuring that our relationship remains a priority despite life's demands.

What do you and your partner do to keep the love alive? Write down your thoughts at the end of this chapter.

However, it's essential to heed the warning signs that you or your partner may not be ready to remarry, such as fantasizing about rekindling past relationships, harboring anger or bitterness toward an ex-spouse, or feeling unable to be honest with your partner.

To summarize, if your spouse has chosen to leave the marriage, remember that you deserve better. Putting effort into a relationship that is no longer mutually fulfilling will only lead to further heartache. Trust that with time and self-reflection, you will emerge from this experience stronger and ready to embrace a brighter future.

NEAR TRAGEDY

AS I REFLECT ON THE TIMELINE, I served Ryan with divorce papers on July 15, 2019, and our divorce was finalized on December 16, 2019. But amidst the chaos of the divorce proceedings another alarming incident occurred, one that still haunts me at times.

At the time of my separation from Ryan, my son was 17 years old, on the verge of entering his senior year of high school. With my daughter away at college for her sophomore year, it was just my son and me navigating life together. We found a small house in our community where we settled for the next year, ensuring he remained close to his school and friends.

Although I had considered relocating to a neighboring town, my son expressed his desire to stay rooted in his hometown, and I fully understood his need for familiarity. Having just endured the loss of his father (in a sense), his home, and the stability he had known for 17 years, I recognized the importance of providing him with a sense of continuity.

The rental house suited us well. Spread across two levels, my son claimed the lower level as his domain, while I managed the kitchen and other shared spaces upstairs. He embraced this arrangement, relishing the independence it afforded him. Moreover, the proximity of our rental to my best friend's home, just three blocks away, provided invaluable support during challenging times.

Around December 11, he began showing signs of a cold. He had a runny nose, but no cough at that point and seemed generally okay. On December 12, I went out to get him some cold medicine to help him sleep better, and he appeared to be coping well.

The following day, December 13, I had a work trip scheduled. Recently appointed as the Head of Marketing for a small online emergency lender, I was expected to attend their annual holiday party at the company head-quarters. Despite my son's cold, he seemed to be managing fine, having even gone to school that morning. Thus, I made the decision to proceed with my travel plans, feeling reassured about his condition.

However, upon calling home that evening to check on him, I noticed a significant deterioration in his health. Unfortunately, the company's head-quarters were situated in a remote Indian reservation in northern North Dakota, making it challenging to secure an early flight back, and my return flight was delayed that Saturday. Concerned about the timeline of my return, I contacted Ryan, who had been staying with his parents since I had asked him to leave our home. and requested that he pick up our son and care for him overnight until my return the following day. Gratefully, he agreed to stay with our son, sparing me the worry of my delayed arrival.

Regrettably, this decision turned out to be a colossal mistake.

At approximately five a.m. on Sunday, December 15, I received a distressing call from Ryan, informing me that our son was being rushed to the local hospital by ambulance. Although I lacked specific details at the time, I later discovered that he had awakened struggling to breathe and immediately sought assistance by contacting his dad, who promptly summoned emergency medical services.

A startling revelation emerged later: Ryan was not present with our son during this horrific moment. Instead, he was purportedly spending the weekend with the former husband of that woman. Subsequently, whether it is true or not I'll never know, but it is my belief that he was actually with her, yet that narrative belongs to another chapter, in a book I will never write. What's pertinent here is that while he did not outright deceive me, he withheld some pretty key information that, had I been privy to it the night before, might have influenced the events of that fateful morning.

What actually happened when I reached out to Ryan on Friday night is he enlisted the help of his father, who retrieved our son from my home. Consequently, on that Sunday morning when our son found himself grappling with breathing difficulties, he was desperately calling out for assistance from the downstairs couch, attempting to rouse his grandparents who were situated one floor above. However, due to their advanced age and deep sleep, they remained oblivious to his distressing cries—a heart-wrenching realization for any parent, leaving me shattered at the thought of my son's plea for help going unheard.

Thankfully, our son managed to reach his dad, who promptly answered the call and summoned medical aid. Racing to the hospital, I encountered an ambulance en route, later discovering that it was transporting my son. Arriving moments later at the emergency department, I was quickly directed to his side.

The scene is still vivid in my mind, a whirlwind of urgency and worry filling the hospital room. Medical staff rushed around, their movements purposeful and urgent. Amid it all lay my son, his eyes wide with fear, struggling to breathe. I rushed to his side, holding his hand tightly, trying to offer some comfort in the chaos. His desperate gaze met mine, and he pleaded with me to have them hurry.

Before I could fully grasp what was happening, they were inserting a breathing tube into my son, a procedure I never imagined for my once-healthy 17-year-old. The doctor explained that his condition was critical, his labored breathing putting him at risk of a heart attack. It was a terrifying realization.

As they worked, the weight of the situation hit me like a ton of bricks. Tears welled up in my eyes, and I clung to the bed rail for support. Two nurses rushed to my side, guiding me to a chair and offering words of comfort.

Despite their efforts, the medical team explained that they couldn't provide the specialized care my son needed. He had to be transferred to another hospital, and I had to make a quick decision. I chose M Health Fairview Masonic Children's Hospital, praying for a miracle as they prepared to transport him.

As the ambulance crew arrived to take him away, I stood frozen, watching as they carefully loaded him onto the gurney. One paramedic climbed up, balancing on the edge with a portable crash cart in hand. The sight sent shivers down my spine; it was a terrifying moment.

That day marked the beginning of a nine-day ordeal in the hospital, battling to reclaim his health.

Ryan and I took turns spending nights at the hospital. I stayed by his side on Sunday night, and Ryan took over on Monday. However, when I returned early on Tuesday morning, the mood was unnerving. His medical team informed me that he had a rough night, and his condition was worsening. They gently suggested that we reach out to our pastor and close family, preparing ourselves for the worst.

How does a parent respond to such devastating news? In that moment, I became like a machine, shutting out the reality of what I had just been told. I immediately called my parents and urged them to contact our church, requesting the presence of one of the pastors as soon as possible. I also asked them to come themselves. It was around eight a.m.

Just a couple of hours later, our pastor arrived at the hospital. Standing around my son's bed were the pastor, Ryan, my daughter who had rushed home from college to be with us, and myself. Together, we prayed fervently. It was in that moment that the weight of the situation hit me, and I realized I might lose my son. I prayed with every ounce of strength I had, pleading with God to spare his life, even if just for one more day. I prayed for his safety and comfort, whether here with us or in the arms of heaven, reunited with any siblings who had gone before him.

What followed next was beyond anything we could have expected. Over the next several hours, there was a noticeable shift. His oxygen levels began to rise steadily, hour by hour. By late afternoon, the doctor delivered astonishing news—our son was defying all odds. His miraculous turnaround had no logical explanation. Not long after, they made the decision to remove the ventilator that had been supporting his breathing for the past three days.

Seeing my son's face again without all those contraptions hooked up to him and down his throat was a moment I will forever treasure. Yet, despite being able to breathe on his own, the doctors soon informed me that his vital signs were declining once more, though not to the dangerously low levels seen before. To assist him, they decided to administer oxygen through a mask, which thankfully proved effective.

Now, you might be wondering what caused this sudden illness in a young man who had been perfectly healthy just a week prior. This all happened around the time when the novel coronavirus (SARS-CoV-2) responsible for COVID-19 first surfaced in Wuhan, China. While it was making headlines, it hadn't yet been confirmed in the U.S.

But it wasn't COVID—at least not that we believe. It took a couple more days before the infectious disease doctor provided a diagnosis. My son was suffering from invasive staphylococcus aureus pneumonia and sepsis, secondary to an influenza B infection. In simpler terms, he was incredibly, dangerously sick.

Today, he still experiences a lingering cough due to the pneumonia that once threatened his lungs, but he is otherwise healthy and leading a normal life. As of the time of writing, he is a college senior, currently engaged in student teaching, with aspirations of becoming a special education teacher next fall.

He persevered. And I didn't lose my son.

The Rebound

THE TRIALS AND TRIBULATIONS OF DATING APPS

I DOVE INTO DATING APPS WAY TOO SOON. After 23 years of marriage, waiting only two months was not enough. While there is no magic number of how long to wait, I think any expert would tell you that two months is a bit premature—two years might have been better.

However, as a writer who had been asked to start writing for an online dating service, I found myself in a unique situation, and not one that most people would run into. I married Ryan in 1997. We met in 1995. I graduated from high school in 1993. If you do the backward math, you will see I was pretty young. I was married by 22! And since the internet was barely a thing at that time, dating apps, if they existed at all, were pretty scarce.

If you are thinking of getting back in the dating game, however, I do encourage you to think about whether you want to start dating again or not. To do this, I recommend asking yourself a few questions before going too far down the dating app path—like before you even sign up.

Am I looking for a plus-one for weddings, or am I ready to find someone who also enjoys binge-watching documentaries in pajamas?

Have I fully accepted that "swiping left" is not a reference to brushing off crumbs from my left shoulder?

Do I miss having someone to share my day with, or am I just bored of talking to my plants—or, in my case, Rufus the dog?

Am I prepared to see my ex on a dating app, and, if so, have I mastered the art of the graceful swipe left? In my case, this was not a risk since Ryan had started an emotionally intimate relationship with What's-her-face before our marriage had even ended. But you must ask yourself how you'll feel if your ex pops up in your recommendations, just in case.

Is my selfie game strong, or do I need a quick tutorial on not looking like I'm about to ask the camera to borrow money? In my case, I became rather smitten with a guy who had his little girl take his dating profile photos for him—more on that later. But seriously, make sure you have some good photos. I have plenty of recommendations on the photos not to include, but that might be a good topic for another book, so I'll hold my thoughts for now.

Am I ready to discuss my boundaries and needs openly, or do I still giggle at the word "intimacy"? And ladies, seriously, this is a big question. If you were married to the same person for a long time, and all or the majority of your intimate relationships were with the same person, don't underestimate how big of a deal this is. While this, too, could be the topic of another book, be sure to take the time to assess your readiness for a new phase of intimacy.

Do I know what I want in a partner, or am I as undecided as when I try to pick a Netflix show?

Am I okay with the idea of virtual dates, or do I still think Zoom is just a camera feature? Even with the pandemic largely behind us, I hear that virtual dating is still a thing.

Will I be able to get through a conversation without referring to the ex and the demise of my marriage? Trust me on this, take one of your girlfriends on a date. Ask her to play the charming man. See what happens. If you find yourself wanting to talk about your ex or struggling to come up with your thoughts without your ex as part of them, you might need more time before taking on a dating app.

Lastly, am I looking for someone to share my life with, or do I need someone to help me finish the leftovers in the fridge?

Okay, you get the gist. Make sure you are ready for what dating app participation implies before signing up. I advise you to review what we discussed earlier in this book about self-love. You need to be able to embrace yourself as a single, independent woman before you venture into the world of dating, online or otherwise. If you don't, you're doing a disservice to yourself and the guy on the other end of the app.

For any single man reading this book and looking to woo a woman on a dating site, I have some advice for you. And I pray that you will heed it:

Don't start your profile with "Just ask." This isn't a game of Twenty Questions, and mystery is less sexy than you think (when it comes to dating apps). Give me something to work with here!

Refrain from tooting your own horn. While it's fantastic that you think highly of yourself, let's keep the self-praise to a minimum. Statements like "I'm a catch," or "Your search ends here," tend to come off as a bit... presumptuous. I'll judge how amazing you are, thank you very much.

Avoid the financial boast. Announcing that you can "financially provide for all my needs" isn't as attractive as you might think. Many women value independence and empowerment over finding a sugar daddy. I'm one of them. Let's focus on emotional connection rather than bank accounts.

Steer clear of the "looking for a mother for my children" line. It's lovely that you're a dedicated dad, but remember, a partner is not a nanny or a substitute mom. Expressing a desire for someone who's a positive, loving influence is excellent, but let's not hand out parenting applications. Plus, as a mom myself, I don't ever want to step on the toes of your kids' biological mom.

For the love of all things holy, skip the shirtless selfies. Unless you're secretly Ryan Reynolds or Justin Hartley (and let's face it, you're probably not), save the six-pack reveal for a more appropriate time. I know that I said earlier that mystery is not sexy when it comes to dating profiles, but leaving a bit of mystery here, is indeed sexy. Let us discover your sexiness later, when the time is right.

Ditch the fish pictures. Yes, we're thrilled you caught a big one, but unless you're a professional angler, maybe leave the trophy fish out of your profile. Believe it or not, holding a bass isn't the aphrodisiac you think it is. And if you take me fishing, let's be clear that I will not touch the fish or the worm. That's on you, buddy.

No ex-bashing. Using your profile to air grievances about your ex is a big red flag. Focus on the future and what you're looking for, not the past.

Keep the adventure clichés to a minimum. We get it; everyone on dating apps loves to travel, hike, and live life to the fullest. Share something unique about yourself that doesn't sound like a cookie-cutter profile.

The car selfie—just don't. You won't impress me by trying to imply you drive a bad-ass car—I drive a bad-ass car. There's more to you than your vehicle's interior. Plus, safety first—let's not glamorize distracted driving.

And, finally, humor is your friend, but try not to overdo it. A witty comment or two can make your profile stand out, but a whole stand-up routine can be overwhelming. Balance is where it's at.

MEETING THE REBOUND

IT WAS LATE AUGUST 2019, shortly after my son and I had settled into our rental home, that I received the message through a freelancing platform to write dating-related content. As you can imagine, I had no idea what to write about, especially with regard to online dating. I had been married for nearly 23 years, and I don't think dating sites existed when I got married back in 1997.

How could I write an article on the topic without experience? I didn't want to write the same article that existed on other sites. I wanted this article to be unique and stand-alone. So what did I do? I created a dating profile for myself on eHarmony.

I went through the process of creating a great profile. I laboriously searched through photos to find the best ones to add. And I painstakingly scrolled through profile after profile of men, looking for love. I quickly learned what I liked to see in a profile and the types of photos that resonated with me. Before I knew it, not only had I written those first two articles, but I had built a pretty robust profile.

I waited. And I waited. And nothing. After two weeks of nothing, I was beginning to feel that dating sites sucked. How could absolutely nobody be interested in me? I was successful in my career, I was well-educated, and I was a great mom. What was wrong?

In truth, the answer is that nothing was wrong. Finding a relationship on a dating site can take time. Yet, I was becoming more and more distraught; those feelings of rejection from my marriage and subsequent separation as we went through the divorce had risen to the surface.

So, when I suddenly got a hit from an interested and good-looking guy, let's call him Mark, I was elated. I was overjoyed that someone found my profile to be interesting. We started messaging one another, and we exchanged telephone numbers before long. And then he called.

He seemed like a pretty nice guy. He was articulate, friendly, the same age as myself, and interesting. He was also a retired police officer. He was retired because he had been diagnosed with multiple sclerosis (MS) a few years before and was going through his own divorce from his wife of 17 years.

I desperately wanted a man interested in me, so I brushed aside the caution I would generally exercise in entering into a relationship so quickly. But in reality, I didn't know what I didn't know. I had no idea the repercussions of an illness such as MS.

Dating someone with MS can be both fulfilling and demanding. While it can bring joy and contentment, navigating the condition's challenges requires patience, understanding, and adaptability.

Mark's MS presented significant hurdles that I hadn't anticipated. His short-term memory struggles were evident, often leading to repetitive questioning and difficulty in retaining recent information. Tasks such as remembering names or daily chores became arduous for him, impacting our day-to-day interactions.

Moreover, his balance issues, particularly challenging given his towering height of 6'5", added another layer of complexity. Walking became a precarious endeavor due to MS-related fatigue, nerve damage affecting coordination, and muscle weakness. These physical limitations made planning outings or even mundane activities a logistical challenge.

Additionally, Mark's PTSD from his time as a police officer compounded the situation, intensifying with the progression of MS.

Nightmares, exacerbated by alcohol consumption, and unpredictable emotional outbursts characterized by intense emotions and foul language, created tense and uncomfortable situations.

Furthermore, his chronic fatigue, whether stemming from MS or medication side effects for depression, disrupted our plans regularly. His propensity to oversleep, coupled with delays caused by impaired coordination and memory, strained our schedules and added pressure to an already demanding lifestyle.

Despite the challenges, I found myself drawn to Mark, craving the affection and companionship he offered. In hindsight, my eagerness for love may have overshadowed our relationship's red flags and difficulties.

Have you ever been in a rebound relationship? Are you in a rebound relationship now? Write down your thoughts and feelings. How will you move forward and put yourself first?

THE ALLURE OF COMFORT AND CONTROL

BUILDING A RELATIONSHIP WITH MARK was interesting, to say the least, and full of ups and downs. As I shared in the previous section, Mark had multiple sclerosis (MS), a condition that affects motor areas as well as how a person thinks and feels. About half of MS patients experience memory, attention, or decision-making problems. Mark had these issues, too.

Sometimes, he'd forget things we talked about, or he'd ask me the same question over and over. It wasn't his fault; it was just part of how the disease affected him. MS can mess with parts of the brain that control mood, making emotions like depression and anxiety, as well as mood swings, more common. This can make relationships tricky because it's hard for others to understand what someone with MS is going through.

When you lose the ability to live independently and see the world the way you used to see it, it can lead to feelings of anxiety and depression. It creates a sense of loss for what you once had. And with short-term memory issues, it can seem like you are reliving that loss over and over again.

For Mark, these emotions often manifested as foul language, even in inappropriate situations. He struggled to read social cues, so he didn't always know when to swear or when not to, which made things awkward, especially around other people.

Despite the challenges, our relationship had moments of comfort and affection. Mark could be really loving and attentive, which I craved after feeling neglected in my previous marriage. His expressions of love made me feel valued and appreciated, even if they were sometimes overshadowed by his outbursts or controlling behavior.

Speaking of control, that was another issue we faced. MS can affect how a person thinks and behaves, sometimes making them more controlling or irritable. Mark often tried to tell me what to do or how to parent my kids, even though he had his own struggles. It was frustrating and made me feel like I was losing myself in the relationship.

Feeling judged during my relationship with Mark was a constant struggle. I could sense the disapproval from friends and family, who couldn't understand why I stayed with someone who caused so much stress and turmoil.

But they couldn't truly grasp what I was going through. They hadn't experienced the same emotional rollercoaster, the conflicting desires for affection and stability. It's easy to judge from the outside, but you can never fully understand someone else's choices or motivations.

Mark had entered the picture when I was deep in turmoil, offering the affection and attention that I had longed for. After years of feeling neglected and unloved, his gestures gave me hope in the darkness. I craved the feeling of being wanted, of being seen and valued. I failed to see the subtle signs of control creeping into our relationship. Mark's actions, once comforting, began to feel suffocating as he asserted his dominance, even dictating how I should raise my children.

In retrospect, I suppose this was because he was losing control of his own thoughts and feelings. The result was this intense desire for him to control whatever, and whoever, he could.

REALIZING THE NEED FOR CHANGE

DESPITE MY DOUBTS AND THE CONCERNS of my friends and family, I stayed with Mark for 14 months. Looking back, I realize I sought comfort and validation in all the wrong places. I wanted to feel loved and desired, but I sacrificed my happiness and independence. And I sacrificed relationships with family and friends—most importantly, my children.

Unfortunately, I realized I needed to make a change long before I did so. By nature, I'm a rather decisive person. I either like something, or I don't. I either do something, or I don't. I don't tend to hem and haw over decisions. While this trait has typically suited me well personally and professionally, it worked against me here.

I had jumped into that relationship with Mark with so much gusto. Truth be told, I hadn't felt love from a man—including my ex-husband— in so long that I'll admit I was desperate. I wanted to follow through with the decisions I had made, including having him move in with me and my son at our rental house and then purchasing a home together a few towns away, just a few short months later.

While I hate to admit it, even to myself, I regretted buying a home with Mark long before we even signed the mortgage papers. I knew my anxiety was at an all-time high—even higher than it had been for those last few months of my marriage. But I felt like I was riding in a runaway train. I didn't know how to jump off. And I was afraid of the embarrassment and shame of admitting I had made a mistake.

So I went on with things. We bought a house together on the northeast side of the Twin Cities. I loved the home. Mark loved the home. But every day, I started to realize more and more what life would be like living with Mark and his MS. To this day, I still feel some shame in not continuing to stand by his side. But it was so hard.

I was largely on my own. I planned the grocery shopping and the grocery delivery orders. I coordinated paying our bills. I cared for our home. I cooked the meals. And as time went on, I realized that Mark either could not or would not contribute to the responsibilities of home ownership. Additionally, since he tended to sleep so much during the day, I grew lonelier and lonelier. And more and more anxious.

We had only lived in that home for three months when I realized it just wouldn't work. Our relationship had become more and more challenging with each passing day. The need to pause from my workday to repeat things to him repeatedly because of his short-term memory tested my patience. The lack of time to truly relax because I was working full-time plus freelancing on the side, then cooking and managing our home, was becoming too much. And I desperately missed my friends and family.

After a sizable argument with Mark, I finally told him I wanted to end the relationship. I started looking for homes back closer to where I had lived before. I was on a mission—to find a fantastic home that would suit me and my son. Even though my son would go to college the next month, I had grandiose visions of him and me against the world. The home I would find would have a room for my daughter so she could visit when she got home from college. They truly were the best-laid plans.

But then I made a mistake—again. As I write these words, I realize just how desperate I was. Mark came to me with a sizable apology, promising to change. Further, he agreed to attend counseling with a therapist skilled in working with those with PTSD and other neurological illnesses. He promised it would get better.

And I believed him.

I got lucky and found a stunning home just one town from where my ex-husband and I raised our kids. It was a floor plan I had seen years ago when walking through homes during the Parade of Homes tour. And it was the perfect floor plan for our needs.

The main level included the master suite plus two additional bedrooms—one would serve as my office, and the other would be my daughter's bedroom. A gourmet kitchen, laundry room, huge living room, and dining area created a perfect design for Mark, who had trouble with stairs. The lower level included a fourth bedroom, a third bathroom, and a huge finished floor plan that would provide a perfect space for my son to have his own place to get away.

While I had intended to purchase the home on my own this time, somehow—and I still scratch my head about how it happened—we purchased the home together. So just four months after moving to the northeast side of the Twin Cities, we were back south of the river. And I was excited to be back close to my family and friends in a home I loved.

Less than two weeks after we had moved into our new home, I realized the mistake I had made. While relocating was definitely the right thing to do, continuing the relationship with Mark proved to be a mistake.

All the challenges we had experienced together in our previous home resurfaced. But now, I was also managing the ownership of a new construction home. This meant I was largely on my own to navigate all the things that came with purchasing a brand new house— window coverings, landscaping and irrigation, getting a fence and a deck, and so much more. I was overwhelmed.

This time, despite his pleading and promises, I knew the relationship needed to end.

I told him I was done three months after we had relocated, and I made it clear that there would be no going back this time. Just before Thanksgiving 2020, he moved out. A few days later, a moving crew came to take his furniture and things, and it was over.

When the moving truck drove away, I closed the garage door and let myself back into the house. I leaned against the door. And I cried. While I am sure that some of my tears were from fear of the loneliness I worried would return, I also cried for the lost time, the healing that hadn't come, and the return of all those feelings of loss that I had experienced just sixteen months before when my ex-husband and I officially separated.

Yet, oddly enough, after that cry ended, it did not return. I discovered that I had found a new sense of freedom. I had finally come to the time where I would learn to accept what had happened. I could finish grieving the loss of my marriage and could work on myself.

Ultimately, my experience with Mark taught me valuable lessons about self-worth and resilience. Each person's journey is unique, shaped by their experiences, fears, and desires. So, while I may have made mistakes and faced criticism along the way, I know that only I can truly understand the complexities of my own situation. I learned that I deserve to be in a relationship where I'm respected and valued for who I am. And while MS may have played a role in our challenges, it's no excuse for unhealthy behavior or controlling tendencies.

I committed to finding a therapist. I rekindled my relationship with my friends, who had been waiting for me to find myself again. And before long, I found myself starting to heal. I committed myself to exercise and eating healthier. I found new energy and passion for my work. And I took on a few additional freelance clients. Life was starting to look up.

ROCK BOTTOM
AND REBUILDING

WHEN YOU HEAR PEOPLE TALKING about rock bottom, you often hear about alcoholism or drug abuse. You hear stories of profound depression and anxiety. And you hear of people taking their own lives.

While it might be hard for my family, especially my parents and children, to read, I won't deny that there weren't a handful of days when I wondered if it was worth continuing this life. I contemplated how and when but knew that wasn't the right choice. My fierce love for my kids is what made me decide to keep on going.

Rock bottom wasn't a single moment for me. It felt more like a series of waves crashing over me at different times and in different ways. Each wave brought its own challenges, each one testing my resolve to keep moving forward.

The first wave hit me like a ton of bricks. Almost losing my son was a nightmare I never thought I'd face. The fear, the helplessness, the sheer terror of coming so close to losing one of the lights of my life shook me to my core. It was a wake-up call, one that made me reevaluate everything I thought I knew about strength and resilience.

Then, there was moving away with Mark. At first, it seemed like a fresh start, an opportunity to rebuild from the ashes of my past. But as we settled into our new life, the reality of Mark's MS became a constant shadow over our days. I found myself in a role I hadn't anticipated, navigating the complexities of a disease I barely understood. Yet, in a way, dealing with his MS kept me from spiraling. It gave me purpose, a reason to wake up every day and fight, even when everything inside me wanted to give up.

Our second move together was the third wave, and by then, I should have recognized the pattern. I should have seen that our relationship, as much as it had become a part of my identity, was also a significant part of my struggle. My rock bottom was intertwined with my relationship with Mark. Despite the love and care I had for him, our partnership was a source of constant stress and anxiety. It drained me, even as I clung to the belief that I was doing the right thing by staying.

I found reasons to persevere. Being needed by Mark and feeling like I was making a difference in his life provided a distraction from my own turmoil. It gave me a sense of value and worth, even on the darkest days. And in those moments of deep reflection, I couldn't help but wonder if there was a reason for it all. Maybe, just maybe, the universe had thrown Mark and me together not to punish us but to teach us—teach me— about the strength of the human spirit, about the power of love and commitment in the face of adversity.

And so, despite the setbacks, the heartaches, and the pain, I began to see my life in a different light. I was blessed with two incredible children, parents who loved me unconditionally, and a talent that allowed me to express myself and connect with others. My writing, which had always been my escape, became my anchor, a reminder of who I was and what I was capable of. It helped me navigate the stormy seas of my life, providing a sense of direction when I felt lost.

Looking back, I realize that hitting rock bottom isn't just about the fall; it's about what happens afterward. It's about picking yourself up, dusting yourself off, and finding the strength to rebuild, even when all hope is lost. It's a testament to the human spirit, a reminder that no matter how hard the fall, we have the power to rise again, stronger and more resilient than before.

Ultimately, my road through the depths taught me invaluable lessons about love, loss, and the incredible power of perseverance. It showed me that sometimes, the hardest struggles lead to the most profound transformations. And it reaffirmed my belief in a higher power, a guiding force that reminds us, even in our darkest hours, that we are never truly alone.

My life has been a blessing despite its moments of despair, triumph, sadness, and joy. As I continue to navigate the unpredictable waters of life, I do so with a heart full of gratitude, a spirit renewed by the challenges I have overcome, and a soul forever changed by the journey.

FACING AND EMBRACING BEING ALONE

THE MONTHS AFTER MY SEPARATION from my ex-husband in July 2019, our divorce in December 2019, and my ending of that relationship with Mark in November 2020 were a whirlwind. But they were also a time of education. I realized that I had never really been alone. I went from living with my parents to living with my now ex-husband. And I was in a new relationship just a couple of months after we separated.

Throughout my life, I've been recognized repeatedly for my independence and ability to stand on my own two feet. While I love my alone time and am comfortable in the presence of no one but myself, I'll admit I like ending the day with a partner. And this is not a conversation about physical intimacy— that's a book for another time and one I am not well-suited to write.

The truth is that I enjoy being in the presence of others—not large groups— just people who I care about. I like knowing that someone I care about and who cares about me is nearby. If I want to have a conversation, I like knowing there is someone there, even if it means walking across the house to find them.

I learned that I just don't like to be alone. I like having a partner. I like knowing someone is as invested in my success as a human as I am. I like knowing there is a cheerleader out there that has my back.

Why do I share this with you? I want those who have experienced something similar to know and acknowledge that going through a divorce is hard. It's like experiencing a death—a death where you know that person is still alive and thinks so little of you that they no longer want to spend their life with you. That's a harsh reality.

When you have experienced a divorce, one of the things you need to do as part of the grieving process is to embrace singlehood. As you can see from my jumping from my marriage right into that relationship with Mark, this wasn't something I did that well. While I could say, "Oh, the situation was so different because my husband cheated," I know that's not the case.

An article I read in Forbes not long ago mentioned that 27% of divorces1 are due to one person in the relationship stating they were done—yep, that happened to me.[1] While I served him the papers, I was in it to win it until he was not.

But, sadly, 24% of marriages end because of extramarital affairs. That statistic devastated me, especially because that also happened to me. I'm of the mindset that if you are unhappy, you work to fix the problems with your partner. You remember the vows you took in front of your family, friends, and God. You work together. You don't just give up. And you certainly don't build a new relationship with a potential romantic partner while you are still married—and understand that emotional affairs can be just as devastating (if not more so) than intimate and sexual affairs.

Once the divorce papers are signed or one of you moves out, that's the closure. In those early months following my separation and eventual divorce from Ryan, I found myself caught in a whirlwind of emotions, dissecting every moment of our marriage, searching for signs,

[1] Bieber, Christie, "Leading Causes of Divorce: 43% Report Lack of Family Support," Forbes Advisor, Forbes Media, LLC, October 17, 2024, https://www.forbes.com/advisor/legal/divorce/common-causes-divorce/

blame, and explanations. But I soon realized that dwelling on these questions, replaying scenarios, and seeking answers for what went wrong offered me no solace. Instead, it kept me tethered to a past that, frankly, had no future.

Seeking further closure by trying to untangle the knots of your failed marriage is like trying to read a book that's already ended. The story is over, and it's time to put the book down (but don't put this book down—keep reading). The energy and time spent deciphering what went wrong could be better spent rediscovering who you are outside of that marriage. It's about finding your self-worth that doesn't hinge on someone else's approval or affection.

Moving into and accepting singlehood after a divorce is a huge step in the healing process. It's a time for reflection, self-discovery, and, most importantly, learning to appreciate the joys of being alone. After the divorce and the end of my relationship with Mark, I found myself standing at the crossroads of loneliness and solitude. Here, I began to understand the profound difference between being alone and feeling lonely.

I realized that being alone is a physical state, a moment or series of moments when you are by yourself. Loneliness, on the other hand, is an emotional state, a feeling of being disconnected, unloved, or unwanted. Acknowledging this distinction was so important for me because it modified the way I viewed my alone time. Instead of seeing it as this huge empty space to be filled with distractions, I started to view it as an opportunity for growth, reflection, and self-care.

This period of self-reflection is not about self-blame or dwelling on your faults. Yes, in self-discovery, you may recognize areas where you fell short or aspects of your personality that contributed to the marital discord. That's perfectly normal and part of growth. The key is to approach these revelations not with self-criticism but with a desire to learn and improve. Identifying triggers and developing strategies to deal with them makes sure that you don't repeat patterns that may have led to unhappiness in your past relationships.

To manage my newfound loneliness, I took deliberate steps to embrace my alone time as something positive. I began filling my time with activities that brought me joy and allowed for self-reflection—working out each day on the Peloton, researching healthy meal delivery services, and mapping out various three-mile walks in the neighborhood—the latter was something that Rufus, my son's dog, benefitted from greatly. This wasn't about staying busy to avoid feeling the void left by a partner's absence. Instead, it was about engaging in meaningful activities that helped me to heal, one day at a time.

I dove into my freelancing, taking on new topics and more clients to keep my mind active and fulfilled at night and on the weekends. This wasn't just a way to pass the time; it was an avenue for me to improve a skill I was already good at. I was like a little kid giving myself a gold star sticker every time I got great feedback from a client.

Embracing singlehood, however, is not about filling every moment with activities to avoid loneliness. It's about learning to enjoy your own company, to be at peace with the silence, and to find joy in the freedom it offers. This period of life offers a unique opportunity to reset, redefine your priorities, and start anew with a stronger, more grounded sense of self. Not many people get this opportunity, so take it as the gift it is.

I realize that copywriting and becoming a freelance blogger might not be the right outlet for you. However, I think it worked as a pseudo-form of journaling. Ask any therapist, and they'll tell you that journaling is an essential tool for self-discovery and reflection. Writing allowed me to process my emotions, acknowledge my mistakes in my failed relationships, and understand the lessons they taught me—even when I was researching and writing on topics completely unrelated to relationships. It was as though learning little bits about all these random topics gave me these nuggets that made me a stronger person.

Aside from my writing, I consciously tried to spend time outside. For those of you reading this who don't know me, it's important to understand that I live in Minnesota—we have the extremes of extremes when it comes to weather. And when Mark left? It was the middle of November—it was cold outside.

But I didn't let that stop me. Because we were still caught up in the end of the pandemic and in-person community walks and 5ks were not yet happening again, I took to the internet to find "virtual races" that I could participate in. I would order the gear, hop on Amazon to order a doggie sweater for Rufus, and would not allow myself to hang my new medal until the two of us had completed our 5k walk (I'm not much of a runner, but it is exceptionally tough to run with a basset hound who tends to trip on his ears).

We (or I, but I like to give Rufus some credit since we were in it together to win) found joy in identifying new 5k routes in our new neighborhood. I loved the thrill of finding a new trail or new turn we could take that would help us discover something new. These moments of solitude outdoors, even in the thirty-degree and below weather, helped me appreciate the present and find joy in the simple things.

This period of self-discovery was not about erasing the past or the person I was before. Instead, it was about acknowledging that I had changed. Ann, who had been married to Ryan, was part of my story, but she was not the entirety of it. I was now just Ann—my own person, defined not by whom I was with, but by my own values, dreams, and aspirations. My life was mine to shape, influenced by my past but not anchored to it.

Celebrating who you are is central to embracing singlehood. Each of us brings something unique and beautiful to the world, and we need to recognize and celebrate these qualities in ourselves. It's about acknowledging our strengths, kindness, talents, and all the good we do. This isn't just an exercise in enhancing our self-esteem—it's a fundamental step in preparing yourself for a future where you can love and be loved in return. The ability to love yourself gives you the building blocks for healthy, fulfilling relationships in the future.

"Ways I will show myself love"

Rediscovering myself also meant learning to be comfortable with my own company, enjoying the silence, and finding strength in solitude. It was about understanding that being alone did not mean I was lonely. I had my family, my friends, and a community that supported me. They were only just a phone call or a text away. More importantly, I had myself—my strongest ally and a constant source of comfort and encouragement.

For those navigating the aftermath of a divorce or the end of a significant relationship, my advice is to give yourself permission to grieve, to feel the full range of emotions that come with such a profound loss. As you venture down the path of singlehood, remember that this road—or bumpy trail—is as much about healing as it is about discovery. You're not just moving away from something; you're moving toward a new phase of your life. This is your time to shine, to explore, and to grow. It's a time to build a life that reflects who you are now, not who you were in the past. Use this period to rediscover who you are, to learn from your experiences, and to grow stronger. Don't make the goal about rushing into another relationship to fill the void—remember my mistake with Mark. Let yourself become whole on your own, find happiness within yourself, and know you are enough.

Facing the reality of being alone taught me that solitude can be a powerful companion on the road to self-discovery and renewal. It allowed me to rebuild my life, not as before, but as a reflection of who I am now—stronger, wiser, and fully me. When you fully embrace this chapter of your life, you open yourself up to the possibility of future love rooted in mutual respect, self-awareness, and a profound appreciation for the person you've become.

THE POWER
OF REINVENTION

WHAT DOES IT REALLY MEAN to reinvent oneself, anyway? Trust me, I've asked myself this question many times. After all, aren't you who you are because of nature, more than nurture? As far as I am concerned, the answer is yes—kind of.

My reinvention wasn't about changing who I was raised to be. I'm actually quite proud of the person my parents raised and who I was long before Ryan entered my life. I'm intelligent, purpose-driven, and bound to succeed—right? Of course I am! But, I'd be lying if I didn't say that my marriage to Ryan, and how it ended, didn't test me and nurture changes to my personality.

Marriage to Ryan wasn't easy, but I did love him. And I had been committed to making it work despite all the trials and tribulations we experienced together. Supporting him through some of those trials and tribulations he brought into the marriage would be enough to make anyone question who they are, their patience, and what they're willing to put up with.

Being married to Ryan challenged me in ways I never anticipated. It wasn't just the ups and downs of a typical relationship; it felt like I was constantly bracing for the next big storm. It's difficult to stand by someone who repeatedly finds themselves in trouble with the law— okay, it was just three times. But ask me how often I have gotten in trouble with the law aside from a speeding ticket here or there over 23 years—never. The experience strains not just your patience but also your understanding, compassion, and even attraction to the other person.

Each incident, each mistake, and each apology from Ryan wore on me—not just as his partner but as an individual. Being connected to someone who struggled with severe personal issues made every day unpredictable and, frankly, exhausting. These weren't just minor slip-ups, they were significant disruptions. I felt like I was walking on eggshells, not sure which Ryan I was going to get.

The toll it took on me was substantial. Over time, I began to see changes in myself—how I viewed myself and, sadly but understandably, how I viewed him. Maintaining respect and attraction for someone is hard when you're constantly worried about what mess will need cleaning up next. It wasn't just about the emotional drain or the practical inconveniences but about how deeply unsettling it is to live with someone whose actions reflect poorly on you both.

This constant state of high alert and anticipation of the next crisis left little room for the softer, more affectionate feelings that should sustain a marriage. I became more guarded and cynical—qualities alien to the person I used to be and totally foreign to who I wanted to be. The man I had fallen in love with, the man I believed I would spend my life with, the man I wanted to lean on for love, security, and protection, slowly became a stranger to me. His actions made him increasingly unrecognizable and unattractive.

Living with Ryan, and knowing the parts of him that he struggled with—his impulsive behavior, his disregard for the rules, and his inability to manage his emotional state—made me question everything. Was this what I deserved? Was this the life I was meant to lead? These questions haunted me, nagging at the back of my mind, chipping away at the foundation of our relationship.

The impact on my professional life was just as significant. Trying to maintain a facade of normalcy at work, to keep performing at a high level in an executive-type role when my personal life was anything but stable, was a Herculean task. The stress of managing both fronts was overwhelming. It left me exhausted daily and kept me from pursuing my hopes and dreams.

When the marital separation came and our divorce just five months later, it became a turning point. It forced me to look at who I was and wanted to be. I realized reinvention wasn't about changing my core values or the essence of who I am—those aspects I am rightly proud of. Instead, it was about reshaping my life so that I no longer felt defined by the chaos of someone else's making. It was about setting boundaries, reclaiming my sense of self, and ultimately, recognizing that I deserved better.

Reinvention became my path to liberation. It allowed me to strip away the layers of compromise, disappointment, and diminished self-worth to rediscover the strong and purpose-driven woman I always was underneath.

This isn't to say that the process was easy or quick. I made plenty of mistakes—a lot of mistakes. However, through the process, I learned that while you cannot control others' actions, you can choose how you respond and what you are willing to accept in your life. And I learned it was okay to be clear about your wants, needs, and expectations. It's not about being demanding, it's about owning what you deserve and pushing back on what you will not stand for.

So what exactly did reinvention mean for me? And what might reinvention mean for you? The truth is that it will never be the same for everybody. For me, reinvention meant deciding to put myself first. It meant recognizing that my needs, desires, and well-being had to come before the expectations and demands of others. This wasn't about turning my back on those I loved but ensuring that my voice was heard, my boundaries respected, and my life lived on my terms.

I started by owning my triggers. I learned to vocalize my discomfort clearly and without guilt, saying things like "I don't like that," "that makes me uncomfortable," or "that's not right for me." It was about affirming my feelings and allowing myself the space to express them. This shift was empowering—it meant I no longer muted my discomfort to keep peace or maintain the status quo.

Taking control of my life also meant reevaluating my relationships. I had to ask myself hard questions about why I stayed, why I forgave, and at what cost. Standing by someone because it's the "right thing to do" can sometimes mean betraying your own values and happiness. I had been through the wringer with Ryan, feeling repeatedly embarrassed and let down by his actions. The things I had to accept as "normal" were far from it. No partner should feel they must bear the weight of their spouse's mistakes as a badge of honor or duty.

My vows were said in front of family, friends, and God with the promise to endure through better or worse. But when the "worse" became such a runaway train, I had to consider whether even God would want me to continue in such a turbulent, destructive environment. It was a profound realization that, sometimes, the bravest and most righteous thing to do is to walk away. My reinvention meant I would never have to sink to such depths again, where my spirit and will were continually crushed by the actions of another.

Though sometimes I wonder why I didn't do it sooner, the fact is that I can't go backward in time. When Ryan decided to throw in the towel and made it clear he was no longer interested in our marriage, the next step was clear—I was done. I was so done that I wanted him out of my life and our family home.

Over the following weeks, months, and years, I learned to stop apologizing for my mistakes, particularly the error of staying too long in situations that drained me—like my marriage to Ryan and the rebound with Mark. Acknowledging these as mistakes rather than failures allowed me to learn from them rather than be defined by them. Each error taught me more about myself, my resilience, and how I needed to change my approach to relationships and self-care.

For me, reinvention was about liberation. It was about freeing myself from the chains of past expectations and forging a path forward that was filled with self-respect, self-love, and self-assurance. It meant creating a life where I could thrive, not in spite of the challenges I had faced but because of the strength I had gained from overcoming them.

For anyone looking to reinvent themselves, remember this: It starts with a decision—a decision to prioritize yourself, change the narrative of your life, and take back control. From there, every step you take builds a foundation for a new, empowered version of yourself.

What can I control? How can I respond to what I can't control?

Resilience

DISASTROUS FIRST DATES

WHEN I FIRST SIGNED UP FOR EHARMONY, I didn't get many hits. I didn't give it much time—something I regret. From when I signed up to when Mark and I connected, I don't think it was more than a week or two. So, please, give yourself some time. Even if you are as desperate as I was—though I didn't realize I was desperate until it was too late—let yourself enjoy the process.

Once Mark was out of the picture, I had a different mindset, and I was ready to go on the dating apps again. Of course, we were in the thick of COVID-19, and in-person dating was still a pretty cautious activity, but I wasn't in too much of a hurry to go out and meet these men immediately. So I let myself have some fun with it.

Just remember that if you are talking to someone on a dating app, chances are that they are also chatting with someone else—possibly multiple people. Don't think that a dating app conversation is a sign of exclusivity.

When I returned to the dating apps, I decided to bypass eHarmony. This isn't to say that the app isn't any good. I just had a bad experience with that one person I met, and I had a bit of a stigma on the brain.

I decided that the apps that were right for me were Match.com and Bumble. I paid for memberships with both. But there are other apps to consider, too:

- Bumble is perfect for those who like to lead the dance. Here, women make the first move, making it a great choice if you're tired of unsolicited messages. Plus, it's not just for dating—there's Bumble BFF and Bumble Bizz, too.

- Tinder is the go-to app for a broad spectrum of connections, from fleeting encounters to long-lasting relationships. It is best suited for those who enjoy the thrill of swiping right and living in the moment.

- Hinge is marketed as an app "designed to be deleted" for individuals looking for more meaningful connections. If you're interested in depth and conversation starters that go beyond the superficial, Hinge might just be your match.

- Match.com is one of the OG dating sites now available in app form, and it's ideal for those seeking a serious relationship. If you're willing to invest time (and maybe a bit of money), Match.com offers a more curated approach to dating. And this is the app I used when I met my now-husband, Scott.

- OkCupid has an inclusive atmosphere and detailed profile options. It's fantastic for those who value personality over pictures. The algorithm finds your perfect match based on shared interests and beliefs, whether you're looking for a date, a friend, or something in between.

- Coffee Meets Bagel is good for busy bees who can't be bothered to swipe all day; this app sends you a limited number of potential matches ("bagels") every day at noon. It's best suited for those who want to slow down the dating process and ponder their choices carefully.

- Plenty of Fish offers plenty of...well, fish in the sea. It's great for those who want to dive into a vast dating pool and fish out a connection without too many preconceived notions.

- Happn is all about location, showing profiles of people you've met in real life. It's ideal for city dwellers and those who believe in serendipity in love.

Okay, enough about the dating apps. Let's get into some of my experiences with in-person dating during this next phase of singlehood. Why am I bothering to share? Well, first, to lighten the mood because we've covered some pretty heavy stuff. And I'm also sharing because dating is supposed to be FUN! Even though I might diss a couple of guys here in what I have to say, the chances are that you'll be racing home after your dates to call your girlfriends and do the same.

Over the course of three months, I talked or messaged on the app or via text with about ten guys. Some of these guys were great for first-thing-in-the-morning texts—it's pretty awesome to wake up and see a good morning text waiting for you. Other guys were good for texts late into the evening. Others were sporadic, popping in here or there to continue conversations.

Online dating was fun! After a while, some of those conversations turned into the ultimate question or suggestion— "Let's get together for dinner." As long as you practice safety first and meet in a public place, I say go for it!

My first in-person date was with Chad. Super friendly and outgoing. He turned out to be a snowmobiler—I grew up snowmobiling—and he invited me to come over and go for a ride. So, I grabbed my gear, tossed it in my car, and drove about twenty minutes to his place to hit the trails for the day. It was a perfect day until he decided to try and get a bit too lovey-dovey in his living room at the end of the night. I pushed him away, and well, that was that.

Next up was Greg. We had lunch together at a restaurant near where Ryan and I had raised our kids. I'll give Greg credit—he checked almost all the boxes. Super polite, personable, entrepreneurial, handsome. But, it was apparent there was no love connection. And he was about two inches shorter than me. As I am only 5'5", this was a no-go. That said, Greg and I actually stayed in touch via text for a couple of months. I hope he has found love—he seemed to be a great guy.

Then there was Chris. Oh, he was so sweet and super friendly in our messages. But when we met in person, the poor guy was so shy he could barely talk to me. He was nervous, that was for sure. Sweaty palms and brow, the whole deal. And while I knew it was not a love connection right off the bat, he totally lost me when he told me he was a father and had no relationship with his kids. For me, that was a deal-breaker. And I suspect that for most moms, this will be a dealbreaker, too.

Almost last but not least was Mike. This guy was a local firefighter, and I'll admit this sounded fun when we first connected. I mean, seriously, a man in uniform? And we had some unorthodox text exchanges. But when we met in person? I had only wished I had asked in advance for the hostess to rescue me should I throw a signal her way. This guy was vile, crude, and everything in between. It was apparent that Mike had no respect for women. He made it clear that women were intended to be sexual objects, and he proceeded to tell me, a woman, how women want this or that throughout our dinner. Boy, was he wrong!! And I'm sure he'll remain single for the rest of his life.

And then there was Scott.

FINDING HOPE IN THE MIDST OF A PANDEMIC

AS YOU CAN SEE, I HAVEN'T SHARED too much about Scott. And that's not for the reasons you might think. I left out those details because, well, today, I wear his last name, and I am proud to do so. We met in February 2021, and were married in February 2023. In fact, as this is being written, we just celebrated our first wedding anniversary a couple of months ago.

I am choosing to leave out those details because they don't matter. And I want to honor the privacy and sanctity of our marriage. But I will tell you that Scott came into my life when I least expected it, proving that, sometimes, the best things happen when we're not looking for them. By no means am I saying Scott is perfect—far from it. But then again, who is? What makes our connection unique is not the absence of flaws but the presence of understanding, acceptance, and shared values.

When we met, Scott had his own set of pains, fears, and worries. He had experienced heartbreak and was fiercely protective of his little girl, who, I am proud to say, is now my lovely stepdaughter. And our path to where we are today wasn't easy by any stretch. We experienced plenty of frustrations. What made this relationship different was that, as frustrated as we might be, we gravitate back to each other, not only to talk it out, but to offer support to each other for the pains and fears that we still felt from our pasts.

Our road together has taught me much about love, partnership, and what it means to find "the right person."

Are you in a thriving relationship? What traits do you value in a partner? Take a moment to reflect and jot them down at the end of this chapter.

So, how do you know when you've found the right person? It's not always an earth-shattering revelation; sometimes, the quiet moments of understanding and the ease of being together tell you. Here are some things I discovered as Scott and I spent more and more time together.

- We didn't always need to fill the air with conversation.
- We respect each other's opinions, dreams, and boundaries.
- We love to laugh—and Scott has this uncanny ability to make me laugh, even when I might be mad or frustrated with him.
- We are aware of each other's flaws and accept them without judgment.
- We both understand that life is not always smooth sailing.
- We inspire and encourage each other to grow, not just as partners but as individuals.
- Trust is the foundation of any strong relationship but when you've been through a challenging relationship previously, triggers can pop up when you least expect them. Scott and I work together to navigate those triggers as they arise.

- While you may have different hobbies or interests, alignment on core values and life goals is necessary. We share similar values, making it easy to create a home together.

- While physical attraction is essential, emotional intimacy is what sustains a relationship. Scott understands my love languages and does his very best to prioritize that my needs are met, and I do the same for him.

- Lastly, when you're with the right person, there's an undeniable sense of being "home." It's a feeling of unconditional love, security, and belonging.

I found these qualities and so much more in Scott. Our relationship is not without its challenges, but our willingness to face them together makes us stronger. He's not just my partner; he's my teammate, confidant, and best friend. Our story reminds us that love can be found in unexpected places and times. And when it arrives, it may not be in the form we anticipated, but it will be exactly what we need.

What are my core values (for myself and my partner?) What are my non-negotiables? How do I "fill my cup"? How will that work in my desired relationships?

THE TURNING POINT: OUR FIRST WEDDING ANNIVERSARY

SCOTT AND I WERE NEARING OUR FIRST wedding anniversary when I started working on this book. And while we have a strong marriage, it hasn't been without its challenges. Many of those challenges have come from trying to blend our two lives together.

We haven't had the luxury of growing up together like young couples do. We lived decades and decades of life without each other— now we had to find a way to bring it all together. The task of blending two established lives into one existence can bring unexpected hurdles despite our strong foundation and shared values.

One of the first logistical challenges we faced was combining two households, each with its lifetime of possessions, memories, and routines. Deciding what stays, what goes, and how to organize our shared space was a delicate negotiation, especially since I was moving into the home he shared with his daughter. We had to be mindful and respectful of each other's attachments to certain items and find a balance that felt like "ours" rather than "yours" or "mine." And we had to find a way to help me feel like it was my home, not just theirs—a challenge that still creeps up from time to time, today.

Scott and I brought children into our marriage but were creating a union that would never produce a child of our own. Blending families presents complexities, especially when one person has adult children and the other has a young elementary-aged child. We would never be in a situation where we truly parented together, but we needed to learn to respect the pre-existing parent-child relationships and find our roles without overstepping.

Combining finances can be particularly tricky for those who have managed their money independently for decades. And, as we each had financial obligations to our existing children, it made this even more tricky. For us, it meant combining 401(k)s, life insurance, etc., but keeping our funds separate.

At our age, health considerations take on greater significance. We're not that old, but we're not spring chickens. We've had to navigate doctor visits, health routines, and sometimes dietary changes to support each other's well-being while maintaining our own. It's about more than just living together; it's about planning for a future that includes possible health challenges and ensuring we are each other's support system.

Merging our social lives was another hurdle. We both had established circles of friends and social routines. I love to spend time with my circle of girlfriends. He's more of a homebody and doesn't need those regular connections. Finding a balance between maintaining these individual relationships and building new ones as a couple requires effort and understanding. What might work for you might not work for us, and vice versa.

Adapting to each other's daily routines and lifestyles has been an exercise in patience and flexibility. And sometimes even the little things such as when we each want to go to bed, or when we each like to get up in the morning. I mean come on, the best thing about self-employment? I can get out of bed whenever I want without anyone to answer to except myself. And what about meal preferences? He can eat anything under the sun and keep a lean body. Me, on the other hand? I look at a cupcake, and I can gain five pounds.

Finally, we faced the challenge of creating our own traditions. After decades of individual habits or habits built in our previous relationships, not to mention holiday routines, we needed to create new traditions to celebrate our life together. This meant blending elements from our pasts and creating fresh practices that were uniquely ours. But it also meant recognizing his approach to holidays and traditions with his daughter, which might not align with my own approach from when my kids were young.

These challenges have taught us much about compromise, respect, and love. We learned that marriage is about adjustment and understanding at any stage of life. Each challenge we faced and continue to face has strengthened our relationship and deepened our bond.

As we continue to move forward, we find joy in the life we are building together, cherishing that we have found each other, regardless of the timing. This realization—that it's never too late for love—has become a central theme of our life together, and it's a message I hope to pass on through the pages of this book.

As Scott and I continue to navigate our married life, we do so knowing that while the road may not always be smooth, it is ours to travel together.

EMBRACING FULL-TIME FREELANCING

MANY YEARS AGO, I took a StrengthsFinder quiz through Gallup. Now called the CliftonStrengths assessment, the intention is to help you understand how you approach your work and how your various strengths might help you do something a bit differently than others. The assessment looks at how you compare against 34 unique strengths. Rather than looking at weaknesses or areas of opportunities, the assessment simply implies that you leverage some of these strengths more often than you might leverage the remaining strengths on the list.

When I took the assessment, I was informed that my top five strengths were: *achiever, learner, discipline, arranger, and competition*. And interestingly enough, my two lowest strengths were ideation and woo. So, what does this mean? And what did it tell me?

Let's start by discussing the ***achiever*** in me. This strength is all about my inherent constant need for achievement. Every day, I feel compelled to accomplish something tangible. It's why I carry around a notebook to help me keep track of not only my open client projects but even some of the most minor tasks that I need to take care of in my personal life—like making my car payment, following up with one of my kids on something, etc. In freelancing, this translates to a relentless drive to meet deadlines, exceed client expectations, and continuously take on new projects to feel successful and productive.

> Have you taken the StrengthsFinder test? What are your strengths? Write them down here with thoughts on how you can leverage those strengths to help you persevere when times are tough.

Next up is *learner*. This is all about my insatiable desire to learn and continuously improve. With its ever-changing demands and technologies, the freelance world provides the perfect playground for a lifelong learner like me. It keeps me engaged and always looking for new skills to master and new knowledge to absorb. And because I have the opportunity to write for clients across a pretty broad variety of niches, I get to learn a bit about a lot of things—it totally plays into who I am.

To be honest, when I first received the list of my 34 strengths in order, I was a bit dismayed to see that *discipline* was in the top five. I worried about how that would make me look to others, especially when I had received feedback throughout the years about being too work-focused and skipping over pleasantries in meetings. But the truth is that this strength simply indicates a preference for structure and organization. Freelancing can often be chaotic and unpredictable, but my disciplined approach allows me to manage my time effectively, set clear objectives, and keep my workspace and workflows organized, increasing my efficiency and productivity. Without discipline, this actually might not be the right career for me.

Being an *arranger* means I can organize and juggle multiple tasks efficiently. This skill is invaluable in freelancing. It allows me to handle various projects simultaneously, shift resources and priorities as needed, and always find the most productive configuration of my workload. But, it also requires me to put up some boundaries in how I approach my work. While some might think these are barriers, I view my boundaries as a way to deliver my best work to each client, every day.

Finally, my *competitive* nature drives me to strive to be the best at my work. Freelancing means continually improving my services, staying ahead of industry trends, and ensuring that my work stands out in the market-place. It means staying purpose-driven while keeping that scarcity mindset at bay. It reminds me that you can't wait for the work to come to you in the freelance world. You need to go out and find it—each and every day.

It might make sense here to share that I had taken the Myers-Briggs personality test many years before participating in the Gallup Strengths-finder assessment. The test returned and told me I am an ISTJ, which stands for Introverted, Sensing, Thinking, and Judging. This personality type is often described as "the Logistician," marked by a dependable, dili-gent, and strong sense of duty.

ISTJs are methodical and meticulous, qualities that greatly enhance my freelancing career. My introverted nature favors deep, focused work periods without the need for constant interaction, which suits the often solitary nature of freelance work. The sensing and thinking make me practical and realistic, grounded in facts and logic—essential for making sound business decisions and delivering high-quality work. Lastly, my judging trait helps me to plan my work and work my plan, adhering strictly to schedules and deadlines. Sounds a lot like those CliftonStrengths findings, doesn't it?

These attributes from the CliftonStrengths and Myers-Briggs assessments were instrumental in my decision to embrace full-time freelancing. While many people might toss aside findings from such assessments, I embraced them. They gave me a way to celebrate that I had talents and skills to offer the world professionally, even when my personal life was going a bit haywire.

These insights reassured me that my natural inclinations and developed skills were well-suited to a freelancing lifestyle. Furthermore, these strengths were critical in my broader path toward reinvention. By aligning my career with my inherent strengths and personality, I've found success, satisfaction, and a profound sense of fulfillment in my work. It has allowed me to live a life that is genuinely "mine", where I can continuously evolve, meet my high standards, and conquer new challenges—all on my own terms.

But what does this mean to you? Why should you care? By no means am I suggesting that if you experience some of the struggles that I did, you should jump into a freelance blogging and copywriting career. If that isn't your talent, you'll indeed crash and burn.

Have you taken the Myers-Briggs personality test? What were your results? What have you learned about your personality type that can help you persevere when things are looking bleak? Jot down some thoughts at the end of this chapter.

But what I am telling you is that you have a talent or skill in you that is just waiting to be discovered and leveraged to help you become a better version of yourself. And when things are looking bad and you're feeling down and out, that might be the best time to try and figure out what those hidden talents are.

During tough times, it's easy to feel lost, unsure where to turn or what to do next. This is why developing new skills or honing hidden talents can be transformational. It's a healthy distraction from the stress and challenges of daily life and a way to inject new energy and purpose into your routine.

For many, tough times trigger a survival mode, leading to stagnation or retreating into comfort zones. I was there, too—going to bed early, sleeping late, avoiding interactions with family and friends. This is natural, as uncertainty tends to push us toward what feels safe and familiar. However, embracing the opportunity to learn something new or improve existing skills can shift this dynamic.

Let's consider the practical benefits first. Learning new skills can open up unexpected opportunities, professionally and personally. Whether it's learning graphic design, a new language, or even carpentry, each new skill increases your marketability. It keeps your brain active and engaged, pushing back against the listlessness and dissatisfaction that often accompany difficult periods in our lives. Moreover, the process of learning can improve mental health by providing measurable goals to achieve, offering a sense of progress and achievement. For me, getting lost in my writing gave me a healthy escape. And with each article I completed, it met that need for achievement—allowing me to check accomplishments off my to-do list.

What skills do I feel confident in? How can I use those to my advantage?

On a deeper level, focusing on personal growth during challenging times can significantly shift your perspective on your situation and capabilities. It provides a sense of control when things around you may seem uncontrollable. For instance, when I dedicated myself to mastering the intricacies of freelance digital marketing, not only did I add a valuable skill to my résumé, but I also regained a sense of agency that the chaos of my personal life had eroded. Each new project I completed successfully was a step toward reclaiming my confidence and independence.

This development of skills and talents also serves as a powerful reminder of your own potential. It's a practical demonstration that growth and change are always within your reach, that you can direct your path, no matter the obstacles. This realization is super important during low points when your abilities and worth might feel overshadowed by your circumstances.

Moreover, engaging in this personal development can connect you with like-minded individuals or communities. These connections can be sources of inspiration, support, and motivation. They remind you that you're not alone in your journey and that others have faced similar challenges and have used these opportunities for growth as a lifeline. For me, it was joining a networking group of other female entrepreneurs. Once a month, I could let my guard down, knowing that every woman in that room had my back.

Learning and developing during tough times is a serious exercise in self-affirmation. It's a way to tell yourself, I am capable of more, and to prove it through action. Remember those words from Aibileen to Mae Mobley: "You is kind, you is smart, you is important."

It's not about ignoring the hard realities of life, but about facing them with a new and empowered attitude. It's about not just surviving but thriving, using your innate talents and newfound skills as tools to carve out a path forward filled with possibilities.

Remember, every challenge you face is also an opportunity to redefine yourself. By focusing on developing your skills and talents, you can transform that time of difficulty into one of success and rebirth.

Note: For those of you who were paying attention earlier in this chapter, I shared my two bottom strengths from the CliftonStrengths assessment. They are ideation and woo. You probably understand what ideation means. And you might understand what woo represents. But, I want to explain these in the context of looking at them as the strengths I leverage least.

Ideation is a strength that revolves around a fascination with ideas, connections between seemingly unrelated events, and the joy of discovering new perspectives on familiar challenges. While many thrive on this constant influx of new ideas and the creative process that it stimulates, my focus tends to be more on execution and practical application than on the generation of new concepts. This doesn't mean that at the time I took the assessment I didn't place a high emphasis on creativity. It indicates my strength lies more in applying ideas than in creating them.

What strengths can you build? Take some time to think about how you can transform your difficult time into something that can allow you to persevere and grow.

Woo, which stands for "winning others over," involves the love of meeting new people and convincing them to appreciate and agree with your ideas or join your cause. It's about making connections easily and enjoying the initial interaction with strangers. In my line of work and personal style, while I value deep, lasting relationships, the process of quickly winning over others is not something I rely on or see as one of my primary skills. In fact, meeting new people gives me quite a bit of anxiety. I have to push myself out of my comfort zone every time I attend a networking event. I tend to focus more on strengthening existing relationships and deepening connections rather than continuously seeking new ones.

Understanding these lower-ranked strengths helps me recognize areas where I might not naturally excel but can still appreciate or develop when necessary. It's not about seeing them as weaknesses, but rather as lesser-used tools in my skill set that I can draw upon when needed, especially in situations requiring rapid idea generation or engaging new networks.

STARTING MY S CORP: A NEW BEGINNING

WHEN I FIRST DECIDED TO GO FULL-TIME with my content writing business, turning that side hustle into an everyday adventure, it opened my eyes to the world of what it takes to truly set up a business. And I'll be honest, it was far more than I had anticipated. Even today, just over a year since formally setting up my virtual shop, I am still learning the things I need to do, and worse, the things I need to redo. All kidding aside, all those mistakes I made in my first year could probably be a great sequel to this book—especially for those who are reading this and thinking of starting their own small business in the gig economy.

If you're not interested in the business aspects of this book, you can skip to the next chapter.

The fact is that when talking to others, I tend to talk about how easy it was getting all those formalities set up—starting the formal corporation with the State of Minnesota, getting my website going, etc. But honestly, all of that was harder than I thought, or at least harder than what I wanted to admit to others.

The steps themselves are relatively simple. But making sure you don't forget anything important is not so simple. I debated for a while on whether or not I would formalize the work that I was doing by setting up a company name, coming up with a logo, etc. After all, couldn't I simply manage my business as Ann Schreiber? The answer is that I could have, but I wanted to give myself the opportunity to grow. I didn't want to get sucked into the limitations of being a sole proprietor in a limited liability company. So, after a long conversation with my accountant, I decided that the S Corp was the better choice for me.

As a quick tangent, for those of you thinking of going into business yourself, you may be wondering about the differences between an LLC and an S Corp. And without getting into too much detail, here's the gist. The differences are all about taxation, ownership, and management.

And to this day, I get asked about this all the time—why did I decide to take the S Corp route? First, if I ever hire employees, I don't plan to have that many. And second, the S Corp will save me on self-employment taxes. Since I am very adept with my recordkeeping and bookkeeping, this was the best choice for me

But that wasn't the only decision I had to make. Over the course of the next year up to where I am today, I amazed myself at the list of accomplishments I have experienced and those things that I have checked off the to-do list. If part of your reinvention is about starting a small business and using your unique talents to help others, you can use the following as a semi-checklist of what to consider.

While the mechanics of setting up the business were straightforward in theory, the practicalities were more complex than I initially imagined. I quickly realized that establishing a solid foundation for my business required careful thought and deliberate actions.

The first critical step was choosing a company name. While I didn't spend an excessive amount of time on this task, I felt a rush of excitement when the name Copywriting For You not only resonated with my mission but was also available according to the State of Minnesota. This name was ideal. It encapsulated my service's purpose—writing that benefits others, helping businesses grow, generating leads, and positioning them favorably in their markets. It was more than a name—it was a declaration of my business's intent.

After registering the name, the next significant task was creating a website. Here, I learned a valuable lesson: never skimp on your digital storefront, whether you are a seller of goods or of services. Initially, I set up my website with minimal thought and strategy, not fully understanding the options available. This lack of foresight proved costly, as I later had to hire a digital marketing agency to overhaul the entire site, something I am still in the thick of now. This experience taught me the importance of investing adequately in digital tools and resources from the outset. Your website is often the first impression potential clients have of your business; making sure it's professional and polished is not something to leave up to chance.

Establishing a rate card was another big step in formalizing my business operations. And I didn't do it right away. I took time to research the rates of other copywriters in the market. I even hired a few copywriters through the Upwork platform to see the quality of their writing for myself. I looked at their rates and the quality of their writing and compared it to my own. I felt fortunate in my confidence that I would increase my rates, knowing that I had a high-quality service to deliver.

That said, it was important to communicate clearly how much I charged and to stick to those rates. As I started increasing those rates for new clients (and asking existing clients to meet me at my new rates), I faced pressure to lower my fees. And while I was happy to grandfather in many of the clients who had helped me get started, such requests from prospective clients were hurtful. Working for less than you are worth can quickly devalue your work and undermine your business's financial health. Plus, when you are truly trying to reinvent yourself, and if you have traveled a similar road to the one I tread, these requests can really mess with your head and how you value yourself.

I likened it to asking them to take a pay cut for the same amount of work and quality— a proposal they would likely not appreciate. All in all, sticking to my guns on pricing not only helped in maintaining my business's value but also attracted clients who respected and understood the worth of good copywriting. And this is something that I talk about a lot today in my business. You'll even see me focus on this point quite a bit if you read my next book: *The Top 10 Mistakes I Made My First Year as a Copywriter*.

Being part of the gig economy, I quickly learned that maintaining the hustle was non-negotiable. Work wouldn't just fall into my lap; I needed to actively network and put myself in front of people who would value my services. This was challenging. From the previous chapter, you know that "winning others over" is not my best strength. However, embracing this aspect of entrepreneurship was a must for building connections, finding new clients, and ultimately ensuring the sustainability of my business.

Continuous learning and skill development were also so important. The field of copywriting and digital marketing is changing all the time, and staying relevant means keeping up with industry trends and technologies. I invested time and resources in taking classes and attending workshops, not only to enhance my skills but also to stay competitive and innovative in a crowded market.

Starting an S Corp and venturing into full-time freelancing was more than just a career change; it was a transformation. Each step, from naming the business to crafting a digital presence, from setting fair pricing strategies to relentless networking, was a piece of the bigger puzzle at play. And the road I am on hasn't just been about building a business; it was about crafting a life that resonates with my values, aspirations, and the needs of the community I serve. It has been about finding a way to appreciate my talents and put them to use.

Are you thinking of using your talents to do something different? Write down your ideas here and come back to them when you are ready to move forward.

Reflections

LESSONS LEARNED AND INSPIRATION

I SHARED WITH YOU EARLIER that the thought of writing this book isn't one I sat and pondered on for a long period of time. It was something that just came to me. And, at the time, it was less about helping others than it was about helping me. But throughout the process of writing, I have found it not only to be cathartic, but I have come to the realization that if I can help just one ordinary woman out there realize that she, too, can get over whatever it is that she is going through and be better for it, than the process will have been worth it.

Ultimately, this book is for ordinary women. There are so many horrible things that people can go through in life. And even though I have gone through some tough times, I know it can be worse. But I also don't want to belittle the experience. Miscarriage, divorce, a super-sick kid? Those are hard things to go through. They change you, whether you want to admit it or not. But those changes don't have to be for the worse. Those changes can make you better. They can make you stronger. They can help you regain control of your life and admit to yourself that you are strong, kind, and important.

You might be asking yourself, what lessons can you learn from such an experience? And the truth is that it will vary from person to person. What

I learned throughout all of this is not necessarily what you will learn. Of course, even though I don't wish my own experiences on anybody, I do know that so many others out there have traveled this same road before. And if that's you, you need to take the time to learn from the lessons. You need to figure out what they are for yourself. And you have to own the decision of moving forward, try to put those hurts and disappointments behind you, and become better for it.

I want to pause for a moment here to be very clear that I am not a therapist, but I have a therapist. I'm still going through this journey myself. It will not ever end. I have to work through 23 years from a past marriage that ended because Ryan felt that I was unworthy of loving. And that's a lot to bite off. But the truth is, I learned I needed to flip the script. I've come to realize that my actions were a reaction to him.

So, I caution you here. Please don't take my words, or anyone's words, for that matter, as the end all and be all to your recovery. I encourage you to seek out help, especially if you find yourself at the bottom of those trenches, wondering how, and if, you should climb out. Don't go through this alone. Lean on those who love you—trust me, the real ones will start pouring out of the woodwork. I have had so many people reach out to me, offering a shoulder to cry on, and a support system to lean on. My parents, especially my dad, were my rock in those early months. My best friend is and has always been my biggest fan and my biggest supporter. And my kids, well, as far as I am concerned, are rock stars of the best kind.

That said, while I've been fortunate to have armies of supporters, I couldn't have gotten to where I am today without some form of professional support. So, I encourage you to be upfront about your experiences and feelings with your doctor. And I implore you to seek out a therapist who can act as that non-partial third party. Remember, your friends are likely to take your side. Your therapist will look at things objectively to help you see what you're doing well, and where you might need some work. And at the end of the day, none of us are perfect. Read that again: None of us are perfect. And it is perfectly okay not to be perfect. Consider yourself perfectly imperfect and lean on that.

With that in mind, consider the lessons that I have learned. You may discover some similar lessons. Yours may be different. That, too, is okay. The goal is to find the lessons. And decide what to do with your new-found knowledge.

These personal trials, such as a miscarriage, a lengthy divorce, and supporting a partner through repeated challenges, were undeniably arduous. Yet, within these heartaches, a series of profound lessons were waiting to be uncovered.

Losing a pregnancy is a profound loss that can deeply affect both part-ners. The grief that follows can seem insurmountable. Yet, it is possible to find lessons even from such sorrow. This experience taught me about the fragility of life and the importance of cherishing every moment. It taught me, after the fact, the value of compassionate communication between partners and the strength of vulnerability. Through this ordeal, I learned that it's okay to grieve openly, to seek support, and to talk about loss rath-er than bottling up the pain. Healing begins when you acknowledge your loss and allow yourself to share in the way that works best for you.

Divorce, especially after spending more than two decades with some-one, can shake the very foundations of your identity. It often prompts the question, Who am I without this relationship? For me, this was a period of intense self-discovery. I learned that my worth is not tied to another person but is intrinsic to who I am. I grasped the importance of setting boundaries and the power of saying no to situations that no longer served my well-being. Most importantly, I recognized the need for self-love and acceptance in the face of rejection.

And let's talk about loyalty. It's a commendable trait, but it can sometimes lead us to accept less than we deserve. Standing by someone who continually tests your limits teaches resilience but should also teach you about your breaking point. For me, I should have known I had reached my breaking point far before Ryan made it clear that he no longer loved me, and, in fact, felt disdain about my very presence. The lesson here is understanding when to step back and put your health—mental, emotional, and physical—first. It taught me that while forgiveness is essential, it should not come at the cost of repeated emotional injury.

Post-crisis, there's a compelling need to establish a "new normal." This doesn't mean erasing past experiences. It's about integrating them into your life to allow you to move forward. It's about building resilience and understanding that you can endure much more than you thought possible. Creating a new normal involves setting new routines, exploring new interests, and, sometimes, forming new relationships. It's about reinvention—deciding who you want to be and how you want to live your life moving forward.

Each of these experiences teaches you about your strengths, limits, and needs. Learning who you are in the aftermath of these trials is not just about recovery. It involves acknowledging that while you cannot change the past, you can influence the future. It's about choosing to use these experiences for the betterment of who you want to be.

REFLECTING ON THE ROAD I NEVER WANTED TO TRAVEL

MY BEST FRIEND AND I RECENTLY REFLECTED on this road that I had never wanted to be on. On our way up to her family cabin in northern Minnesota, we chatted about where we are today compared to who we were way back when. In my case, we shook our heads in disbelief, knowing that it had been almost five years since Ryan and I separated. But even more so, it had been over six years since I had shown up in her driveway, asking her to tell me that my husband was not cheating on me. And it has been nearly seven years since speculation of Ryan's lack of commitment to our marriage had truly made itself known.

This road I have traveled seems overwhelmingly vast when I compare where I was five to seven years ago to where I stand now. Looking back, I sometimes feel like I am observing a completely different person. That old life—my past life—feels disconnected from the person I have become. Yet, that reflection is so important, not for the purpose of longing for what was, but to appreciate how far I have come.

Grieving the life I lost has been a big part of this journey. It wasn't just about ending a marriage but saying goodbye to an entire identity built around a partnership that spanned decades. It's a peculiar type of mourning—one where you grieve not necessarily for a person but for the dreams, routines, and shared moments that once defined your daily existence. I don't necessarily miss the relationship as it was in its final years, but, instead, I mourn the life and the plans we had built together.

This grief also extends to the impact it had on my children. Though they were teenagers and young adults when the separation occurred, the dissolution of their family's foundation was undeniably jarring— this period required us all to redefine our relationships with each other and to develop new dynamics that respected their growth into independent adults while still providing them the support they needed through the turmoil.

As time has passed, reflecting on the road behind me has naturally become less frequent and less painful. Initially, it felt necessary to constantly analyze and reanalyze the past to understand and perhaps find some closure. But over time, I have found that I no longer do that. I've learned that dwelling too long on the roads already traveled can prevent you from appreciating the path you are on now. And thankfully, I have felt myself at a place where I no longer need to fall into that place of analyzing repeatedly.

What on my new path am I excited about?

This doesn't mean I ignore my past or pretend it didn't exist—far from it. Instead, I have learned to view my previous experiences as valuable lessons rather than chapters I wish to erase. Turning these reflections into a constructive exercise has helped me focus more on my current chosen road and less on the one behind me. This shift has been key to my mental and emotional health, allowing me to embrace the present and look to the future optimistically.

In embracing the life I lead now, I've come to celebrate the resilience and strength I've found in myself. It's about acknowledging that while the past shaped me, it does not confine me. Every step forward in this new phase of my life is taken with confidence earned through surviving and thriving past those challenges that once seemed insurmountable.

As I continue to reflect on the road I never wanted to travel, I do so with the understanding that it has provided me with invaluable insights about love, loss, and personal growth. This experience has taught me about the depth of my strength and the boundless capacity for renewal we all possess. Now, I focus on cultivating a life filled with purpose and joy, ensuring that the lessons learned illuminate the way forward, not just for me but, hopefully, for others who find themselves on similar paths by sharing my story.

This isn't just about looking back—it's about using the past as a foundation to build a future that resonates with who I am now and who I still want to become. It's a continuous process of learning, adapting, and evolving.

FINDING STRENGTH IN ADVERSITY

I WANT TO STEP BACK HERE and discuss the adversity you might face during these tough experiences. Sometimes, adversity comes from people and places you never anticipated. No matter where it comes from, it doesn't change the hurt.

Let's start with the miscarriage. Some of you reading this may wonder why I chose to bring this into my story. Well, to start, because it happened. Because it changed who I am, and ultimately, it even changed who Ryan and I were together. When it happened, I had people who actually said to me, "It could have been worse. You could have lost a child that had already been born."

My favorite was from those who told me that because I had never held the baby in my arms, it couldn't have been all that bad. Or maybe the hurt came from the friends who didn't know what to say and then chose not to say anything at all. And I still, to this day, have people who tell me to "get over it." I pray they never go through a similar experience.

The fact is that there is this stigma about miscarriage out there. It's like if you don't speak the word out loud and don't talk about it, it never happens. So, what are you supposed to do if it happens to you? Do you just pretend that the nursery you had started creating in one of the spare bedrooms doesn't exist? Do you write off that your jeans are no longer buttoning to simple weight gain?

It's unfortunate that women going through a miscarriage have to feel any of these hurts and that they have to experience adversity instead of love and support. And it breaks my heart that we have to experience this kind of adversity when we're hurting so badly, mourning the loss of that baby we will never hold in our arms and only in our hearts. If you suffered a miscarriage and have faced this, I know you get it. And if you are reading this and have made any of those comments or felt that a miscarriage really didn't matter, I implore you to think again.

Next, let's talk about the adversity you might face when beginning a marital separation on the path to divorce. In my case, Ryan and I had been married for over twenty years. We had grown up together and made many friends throughout the years. When you separate, it's inevitable that some of those friends will take sides and will disappear from your life, forever. This is challenging. It hurts. In my case, I miss so many people from that past life—good people that I enjoyed knowing. And it hurt even more when people took his side—especially not knowing the things he had done.

Yet, it's important to realize that when you go through a marital divorce, you will also experience a divorce from friends you met along the way. It's part of the experience. You can't stop it from happening, and, ultimately, those friends aren't always worth fighting for. Remember that no one else besides you understands the full story of what happened—so don't hold them accountable for it. Don't expect them to know your ex's mistakes during the marriage. Don't expect them to understand how hard it was for you to play the role that you were in. It's an unfair expectation, and, quite frankly, it will send you spiraling down a rabbit hole that you really don't want to explore.

And now, let's talk about the stigma that people will place upon you when you decide to start dating again. This one was a doozy. It was challenging to hear some of those closest to me make comments that it was too soon to start dating, or ask me if that was really the best thing to do. The judgment that rolled off their tongues as they said those words to me cut me to my core.

There is that line that says, "until you have walked in my shoes" or "until you have walked in their shoes," but the truth is that you will never walk in anyone else's shoes but your own. And they will never walk in yours. So when people cast judgment, it really hurts, especially if they don't, and never will, experience what you have been through.

In my case, only a very small list of people know what I went through in my marriage to Ryan, and I'm not sure I have chosen to share everything. Even my kids don't know all that I tolerated and what that experience was like. And I have decided to keep much of that to myself. Earlier in this book, I mentioned protecting the guilty—and that comment is said as much to keep myself from getting into trouble with what I share about my marriage as it is to keep myself from reliving it, and worse, to admit that I tolerated it for as long as I did.

For others to cast judgment or to look upon you as though you are making a mistake when you move into the dating scene again, it hurts. And it's not what you need. As an adult, you need others to be there for you, to let you make your own mistakes and choose your own successes and failures.

When I think of that relationship with Mark, I know others looked down on me for it. And I understand why—he wasn't the easiest of people to be around. But ultimately, it was a choice I made, right, wrong, or in between. Do I regret parts of that relationship and how long I let it go on? Of course I do. But, I also know that I learned a lot during that time. And honestly, having someone there, anyone, for that matter, helped me to hold on to the little that I had left.

Facing adversity from those who might question or judge your actions after going through something traumatic is an all too common part of healing and moving forward. The only way forward is to find ways to navigate these challenges, especially when the people involved are likely to be in your life for the long haul.

The first step in handling this adversity is to establish and maintain boundaries. It's important to communicate clearly what is and isn't acceptable in terms of discussions about your personal life and decisions. This doesn't mean shutting people out, but rather guiding them on how to support you better. For example, you can express that while you value their concern, you need to make choices that are best for you without external judgment.

Who can I lean on for support, personally and professionally?

Another strategy is to focus on building a support network of people who do understand, or who are at least willing to offer unconditional support without judgment. These might be friends, family members, support groups, or a therapist. Having even a small circle of trusted individuals can make a significant difference in your ability to cope with and rise above the negativity you might encounter.

It's also helpful to remind yourself of your own strength and the validity of your experiences. You have survived and are moving forward, which speaks to your resilience. While it wasn't the right path for me, I have heard others suggest that keeping a journal or engaging in reflective practices can help reinforce your sense of self and remind you of the progress you've made, especially on days when external judgments feel overwhelming.

Also, try to practice empathy toward those casting judgment. Often, people's reactions are more about their own values, experiences, or fears rather than a true critique of your choices. Understanding this doesn't necessarily make harsh words hurt any less, but it can help you to depersonalize negative comments and possibly guide constructive conversations that deepen mutual understanding.

Last but not least, embrace the idea of living authentically. Making decisions based on your true self and your own needs, rather than to appease others, is not only fulfilling but also attracts the right kind of relationships and respect from others. People respect authenticity, even if they initially react negatively to changes they see in you.

In moments of doubt, remember that adversity often breeds strength. Each challenge faced and overcome is a step toward becoming a more resilient and compassionate person. By focusing on what you can learn from these experiences and how they contribute to your growth, you can turn that adversity into a source of power. This approach doesn't erase the pain of judgment or loss but can help you move forward along the path of personal triumph and peace. Ultimately, it's about being and living true to yourself.

What will you do to be true to yourself? What can you do differently than what you are doing today?

ENCOURAGING OTHERS TO EMBRACE CHANGE

ONE THING I LEARNED, that I didn't necessarily expect, was that others needed to go through their own process of accepting this new normal. My family and friends had been part of Ryan and my lives— throughout all of it. So, when that marriage came to an end, it had an impact on their world, too. Things would be different going forward, and they needed time to come along for the ride.

While in those initial months after the separation, there was a lot of love and support, there were also some challenging experiences. Whether it was for the intention of gossip or just because they didn't know better, I would get asked a lot, "Have you heard anything from Ryan?" People seemed to think I would know what he was up to— and even worse, that I actually cared. The constant questions about his whereabouts and what he was up to served no purpose for me. Aside from working through the legalities of our divorce, selling off our joint properties and splitting the differences, my only worry as far as he was concerned, related to my children. If you are riding the tidal wave of divorce, remember to give others time to catch up to you. For many, they may have no idea that things were anything less than stellar in your relationship. In my case, it came as a shock to so many people. While several people in my life knew of some of Ryan's quirks and transgressions, few knew what was going on to the level that it was. And because we were a relatively successful power couple, the reality of the marriage's demise was a devastating shock.

So, understand now that you might find yourself fielding uncomfortable questions or finding yourself the subject of gossip. This can be one of the tougher aspects to manage because, while you are seeking to heal and move forward, some might be more interested in the drama of the situation. It's helpful to have prepared responses for such intrusions. You could say, "I appreciate your concern, but I'm focusing on positive steps forward," or "I'm not comfortable discussing this right now." Setting these boundaries gently but firmly helps others understand your need for respectful interactions.

Moreover, it's okay to explicitly ask for the type of support you need. If gossip or probing questions are hurtful, let your friends and family know. You might explain, "I know you might not realize this, but discussing these details makes it harder for me to move on." In my case, I had to be very specific with some of the people I cared for most by saying, "Your consistent questions and comments about Ryan are hurtful to me. He hurt me, and I need you to either be supportive to my healing, or step aside."

Remember, too, that while your loved ones are adjusting to your new life circumstances, you are not responsible for managing their feelings about it. You can offer information and set boundaries, but their emotional journey is theirs to navigate. Trying to take on the role of counselor or mediator in your own crisis can be both exhausting and detrimental to your healing. Your primary responsibility is to your own well-being and recovery.

It can be challenging when those close to you are processing your situation in real-time, especially if their reactions are strong or emotional. However, it's important to keep in mind that just as you are entitled to your path through recovery, they are entitled to their process of acceptance. It's natural for them to have emotions about the change, especially if they care deeply for you.

Most people don't want to add to your stress and will appreciate the guidance on how they can better support you. As you move forward, remember that you are on a lifeboat heading toward safety. They can either be on the boat helping you to get there, or you can leave them behind— sometimes, you need to choose the latter.

The goal is not to isolate yourself but to create an environment where mutual understanding and respect guide the interactions. This might mean some relationships become strained or even distant for a period. Don't lose focus on your journey. Do not let yourself be pulled into everyone else's emotional responses to your life changes.

As you move forward, your friends and family will likely begin to adjust to the new realities. This adjustment period is important for everyone involved. By allowing them the space to process and by setting clear boundaries, you help ensure that your relationships can evolve in healthy and supportive ways.

SUMMING UP YOUR TRANSFORMATION

WHATEVER ROAD YOU HAVE TRAVELED that has led you to a transformation or reinvention, take some time to develop a summarized version of your story. Who are you today and why does it matter? What have you learned during your own life's journey that has helped you get here? What is your elevator pitch if you were asked?

I'll be honest, this was a challenge for me. During a recent video shoot to help promote my business, the photographer and videographer asked me this very question. I stumbled with trying to come up with the answer. I have been so focused on the roles that I have played that I have had trouble coming up with that short, summarized version. But, I'll give it a try here.

Today, I am not simply a survivor of personal trials such as divorce and significant health crises within my family, but I am also a thriving free-lance writer and a steadfast supporter to those I love. My transformation from someone who once lived in the shadows of others' expectations to someone who now crafts her path with clarity and purpose matters because it is all about the power of resilience and self-discovery.

What's your elevator pitch? Take a few minutes to write down your thoughts at the end of this chapter.

Who am I today? I am a seasoned content creator who not only writes to earn a living but to connect and empower others. My work is not just about forming sentences but about shaping experiences and facilitating connections. It matters because, through my words, I offer support, guidance, and understanding to those who might still be finding their way.

What do I have to offer the world? It is the insight that transformation is not just possible but is perpetually within reach—and when you reach for it, you will find it. I promise, you will find it.

Each piece I write, every story I share, leverages the honesty of my experiences and the lessons they have borne. This is my offering: a voice that champions the potential for change and celebrates the beauty of becoming who you are meant to be.

My elevator pitch? I help translate life's complexities into accessible insights that motivate others to embrace their own journeys of change.

Okay, just kidding, that was a bit of a mouthful.

What is my real elevator pitch? I'm an ordinary woman who has experienced ordinary trials and tribulations, not that much different than what you may have faced. What perhaps sets me apart is that I didn't take those experiences and let them end me. I took those experiences, learned how to heal and cope, and let them teach me how to be a better version of myself, for those I love. But most importantly, for me.

FINAL THOUGHTS ON PERSEVERANCE AND REINVENTION

WHAT DOES IT MEAN to persevere and reinvent yourself? It's about taking all of those bad things from your past and accepting that, yes, they happened. You can't go back and change them. But what you can do is learn from them. Take those failures and all those things and people who hurt you, and let them teach you. Let them help you to become stronger in everything that you do.

This process is fundamentally about transformation. It involves embracing the past, however painful, and using it as a catalyst for remarkable personal growth. Like I said, it's about recognizing that while you cannot change what has happened, you can shape your response to it. Each setback, every heartbreak, and all the hurdles can become stepping stones leading to a stronger, more resilient version of yourself.

Perseverance is not only about enduring the hard times; it's about thriving despite them. It requires a blend of grit, hope, and unyielding commitment to pushing forward, even when the path is obscured by doubt or pain. To those readers who find themselves struggling in the land of adversity, remember that it is entirely within your power to redefine your narrative. The process of reinvention allows you to peel back the layers of who you thought you were supposed to be, revealing who you truly are and, more importantly, who you can become.

Consider the qualities you admire in others who have faced similar challenges—perhaps their tenacity, their compassion, or their unwavering optimism. These are attributes you can find and grow within yourself. Reinvention means taking stock of your values, your passions, and your dreams, and aligning your life with these elements. It's about building a life that reflects your true self, not the expectations imposed by others.

Who do you reinvent yourself to be? That decision is yours alone. It might mean pursuing a new career that aligns more closely with your passions, adopting healthier relationships, or simply learning to see yourself in a new, more empowering light. Reinvention takes you down a deeply personal path, one that might require you to explore uncharted territories within yourself. It allows you to discover strengths you never knew you had.

As you set off on, or continue, this journey, keep in mind that every step, even the smallest one, is progress. Celebrate the victories, learn from the setbacks, and remain focused in your belief that you are capable of extraordinary things. Reinvention doesn't happen overnight, and it isn't always linear. It is a continuous process of becoming, of ridding yourself of what no longer serves you and embracing new possibilities.

Let these final thoughts be a reminder that your past doesn't have to define your future. You have the power to shape who you become. Use your experiences, both good and bad, as the fuel to propel you forward. With perseverance and a commitment to self-discovery, you can transform your life into one of resilience and renewal. Envelop yourself in this story reinvention—it's not just about surviving; it's about thriving as the very best version of yourself.

EPILOGUE

AS I LOOK TOWARD THE HORIZON, I see a future brimming with potential and new adventures. This new road that I am on continues to offer turnoffs that are exciting and inviting, both personally and professionally. As far as my career goes, I am dedicated to further growing my freelancing business, leveraging the lessons learned and experiences gained to expand my services and reach. The challenges and triumphs of the past few years have not only shaped me as a person but have also honed my skills as a writer and entrepreneur.

Reflecting on my professional experience thus far has ignited a spark for my next project—a new book. This forthcoming work will evolve from the deeply personal reflections shared in this current memoir to a more professional focus, detailing the insights and realizations from my initial years in the copywriting and freelancing industry. This book aims to guide and inspire those getting started on their own freelance journeys. I'm hopeful that by sharing what I have learned, and the mistakes that I have made, that I can help them pave a better path forward.

For those of you who have supported me in these recent years, and those who continue to do so, I thank you. And as much as I may be a writer, no words can ever sum up what the role you have played has meant to me. Whether you were my confidant, my shoulder to cry on, my devil's advocate, or just there when I needed you to be, you will never know how significant the impact is that you had on my life.

I am sure some of you reading this, who know me well, will assume credit just goes to my parents, my sister, my kids, and my best friend. But I want you to know that the role you played was important, too. Nearly everyone I have interacted with in these last five years has been a part of my healing journey. Know the impact you made and that you are one of the reasons I am where I am today.

Today, I am facing what I believe will be some of the best years of my life. My children are happy and healthy. My daughter is pursuing a career as a Christian-based psychotherapist and is working with those who have been through traumatic experiences. Whether her experience as a child of divorce has helped her become who she is today, I honestly hope not. But, I know her resilience and her own perseverance will help her to become an amazing counselor. Her kindness, care, and empathy toward others is absolutely remarkable.

My son just graduated from college and has landed his first teaching job at a nearby middle school. He too has persevered through some challenging times—not only the divorce of his parents right before his final year of high school, but fighting for his life and now living with the aftermath of a serious health set-back. And let us, too, reflect on what the COVID-19 pandemic did to all of us, changing the way we see the world, our longevity, and how we interact with others. Through so much change in such a short time, he has become quite my hero. For a while after his father and I separated, it was just the two of us against the world. And his strength not only fascinates me, but inspires me, too.

I am filled with anticipation and joy at the prospect of becoming a grandparent. My daughter and her husband are thinking about starting their family, and the thought of welcoming a new generation fills me with so much happiness. My commitment to being the best mother I can be remains at my core—not only to my own children but also to my cherished stepdaughter. Working through the complexities of a blended family has its challenges, but the love and bonds we have formed are so rewarding and I wouldn't have it any other way.

My relationship with Scott continues to be a source of strength and inspiration. We're continuing to navigate this new life together. We're figuring out our normal and continuing to blend our lives together. Our goal is to create not just a loving and strength-based marriage, but a unity that offers support to my adult children, and his young daughter. Our lives together are about supporting them as much as it is about supporting each other. As we grow together, my commitment to being a supportive and loving wife remains one of my biggest values. My love for him influences my world, and I am determined to make sure it resonates just as powerfully in his.

As I embrace these upcoming chapters of my life, I carry with me the lessons of the past and the hope for the future. Whether it's loving and caring for my family, enriching my writing, or setting off on new and not yet discovered professional ventures, I am committed to living fully and embracing each moment with gratitude and passion. The road ahead is filled with possibilities, and I am eager to explore each one, continuing to write my story with both determination and heart.

ENCOURAGING READERS TO TAKE THEIR NEXT STEPS

I WANT TO OFFER A BIT OF A NOTE and some encouragement to those who may not be as far in this process as I am. If you have recently suffered the loss of a child, whether you had the honor of holding your child or not, I sympathize with you. I feel your loss and the hole it will leave in your life. Lean on your friends and loved ones during this time. Don't feel ashamed of your feelings—own them and the pain that has overtaken you. But know this—you will move forward. You will never forget, the pain will never be forgotten, but you will move forward. And your love for your little angel can help fuel you in getting through future challenges.

For those of you in a bad marriage, or going through the pain of separation or divorce, I am so sorry. I, too, know that when I took those vows, I intended for that relationship to last forever. I understand the pain when it doesn't. But know this—you will move forward. You will never forget, the pain will never be forgotten, but you will move forward. And your love for yourself can help fuel you in getting through future challenges.

For those of you who have had a sick child, whether chronically ill, or with some mysterious illness as what happened with my son, the fear can be overwhelming. The worry of losing your child, your most precious part of you, is agonizing. It ultimately takes over. And I pray that your child will be okay. I pray that you, too, will be as fortunate as I am to enjoy another day with my child—to enjoy all the years that have come and since passed after those days in the hospital.

And know this—you will move forward. You will never forget, the pain and fear will never be forgotten, but you will move forward. And your love for your child, whether they are with you now or gone to heaven, can help fuel you in getting through future challenges.

Whatever you are going through, find the people who will say, andmean—I got you. I will be by your side, your shoulder to cry on, your person to lean on. I am here for you yesterday, today, and every day in the future. These people are your lifeline. Hold on to them and do the same for them when they need you down the road. Support those who helped you to persevere and to reinvent yourself. These are your people. And you are you—reinvented.

What are your next steps? Write them down here and come back to them when you are ready to move forward.

ACKNOWLEDGEMENTS

THERE ARE SO MANY PEOPLE I wish to thank for helping me get to where I am today. Of course, my kids come first on that list. Cate and Zach, it is such a blessing to be your mother. I thank God for you both every day. Thank you for standing by my side, having my back, and being you. You are such a gift.

To my parents and sister, thank you for your support throughout the years. Dad, you were such a support in my early writing by introducing me to that computer keyboard, and just look where I am today, publishing my first book! Mom, thank you for being that Girl Scout leader, soccer coach, prom dress hemmer, and so much more. And to my sister, thank you for everything. There are no words to describe how much you mean to me, and how much I love you.

To my best friend, where do I even begin? Let's just say this—for all the things you have done and continue to do—I love you so. And for all those things I left unsaid—I know you know, and thank you for letting me tell the rest of the story that was left unsaid in this book, to you, and to you alone.

To all my friends including the Classy B's—you know who you are—I hope you know how much you have done for me throughout the years. You have been there through the good and the bad. You are my army, and we all know how every girl needs their army. Thank you.

To my neighbors. Thank you for accepting me into your lives and making me feel welcome here. It's never easy to pick up and move to the other side of town. But now? I can't imagine a life here without all of you.

To my husband, Scott, I love you. Thank you for helping to create this new life we are in. I am so proud to be your wife and to stand by your side. Thank you for encouraging me to start my business, to write for others, and to use my words to tell my story. And to the "little" in our life, I am so blessed to be your stepmom. I love you so much and can't wait to see all the amazing things you will do in this world.

Last but so very not least, thank you to the team at Fox Pointe Publishing. Thank you for helping me take the jump from a self-published author to one with a team here to support me every step of the way. Kiersten, thank you for your leadership and guidance, and most importantly, your belief in me and helping me share my thoughts with the world. To Scotty, thank you for designing the most amazing book covers that help reflect who I am and the stories I have to tell. And to Emma, thank you for having my back and cleaning up my story in a way that makes me proud. I am so thankful to have all of you on my team.

For those I missed, I'm sorry if I didn't provide a callout. The fact is, there are so many amazing people who have come into my life at just the right time, to provide just what I needed. If you are one of those people, thank you, from the very bottom of my heart. Please know you made a difference and continue to do so today.

And to everyone else reading this book, thank you for the opportunity to tell my story.

ABOUT THE AUTHOR

Ann Schreiber is an accomplished freelance copywriter, blogger, and owner of 'Copywriting For You.' She has been in the marketing and sales business for over 25 years and is passionate about business-focused writing.

She released her first book, *Perseverance. Reinvention*, in 2024. Her next book, *The Top 10 Mistakes I Made My First Year as a Copywriter*, will be released in the spring of 2025, which chronicles the mistakes she made during her first year as a small business owner in copywriting and content writing.

Ann received her bachelor's degree in English communications from the University of Minnesota and her master's degree in business communication from the University of St. Thomas. She has two adult children and remarried in February 2023. She is now blessed with a wonderful husband and young stepdaughter as well.

Ann enjoys reading when she isn't busy typing away on her laptop for her clients or for fun. Her favorite authors include Colleen Hoover, Jodi Picoult, and Kristin Hannah. Ann also enjoys spending time outdoors, working out on the Peloton, and taking her son's bassett hound for daily walks.

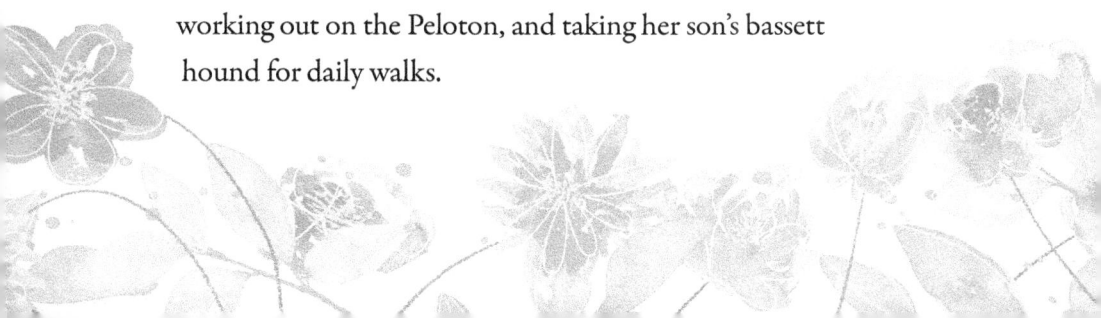

www.ingramcontent.com/pod-product-compliance
Lightning Source LLC
Chambersburg PA
CBHW052021030426
42335CB00026B/3235